Spring and Port Wine

A Comedy

Bill Naughton

A SAMUEL FRENCH ACTING EDITION

FOUNDED 1830

SAMUELFRENCH-LONDON.CO.UK
SAMUELFRENCH.COM

FOR AMATEUR PRODUCTION ENQUIRIES

UNITED KINGDOM AND WORLD EXCLUDING NORTH AMERICA

plays@SamuelFrench-London.co.uk

020 7255 4302/01

Each title is subject to availability from Samuel French,

depending upon country of performance.

SPRING AND PORT WINE

Presented by the Mermaid Theatre Trust and Allan Davis Ltd at the Mermaid Theatre, Puddle Dock, on the 10th November 1965 with the following cast of characters:

(in the order of their appearance)

DAISY CROMPTON	*Ruth Dunning*
FLORENCE CROMPTON	*Jennifer Wilson*
BETSY JANE	*Gretchen Franklin*
WILFRED CROMPTON	*Melvin Hayes*
HAROLD CROMPTON	*John Alderton*
HILDA CROMPTON	*Jan Carey*
RAFE CROMPTON	*Alfred Marks*
ARTHUR	*Ray Mort*

The play directed by ALLAN DAVIS

Setting by ADRIAN VAUX

The play was subsequently presented by Allan Davis Ltd, Michael Medwin (for Memorial Enterprises) and The Mermaid Theatre Trust, at the Apollo Theatre, Shaftesbury Avenue on 3rd January 1966 with the cast unchanged and a setting designed by Hutchinson Scott.

SYNOPSIS OF SCENES

The action of the play passes in the Crompton home Bolton, Lancashire

ACT I
Friday

ACT II
SCENE 1 Sunday
SCENE 2 Monday
(The curtain is lowered during Scene 2 to denote the passing of a few hours)

Time—the present

ACT I

SCENE—*The living-room, kitchen and scullery of the Crompton home. Early evening.*

Most of the stage is taken up by the living-room, which has a bay window down R, a door to the hall up C and one to the kitchen up L. The kitchen also has a door in its downstage wall which leads to the scullery. The scullery extends down L of the living-room wall, and in its own L wall is the back door of the house. The front door is off up R of the corridor C. The house is a comfortable, prosperous, working-class home. The furniture is fairly modern, everything is polished and well cared for. There is nothing cheap or vulgar.

When the CURTAIN rises, the living-room is empty, and a transistor radio is playing on the sideboard up R. DAISY CROMPTON enters from the kitchen carrying six side plates which she lays deftly, humming to the music, on the table RC, giving extra attention to Rafe's place at the head. DAISY is a seemingly contented housewife in the forties. She waves out of the window to Florence, then picks up her worn leather bag from the sideboard, switches off the radio and sits in the armchair C, adding up her accounts and counting money.

FLORENCE CROMPTON enters by the front door, hangs up her raincoat in the hall and enters the living-room carrying a briefcase. She is a teacher, in her twenties, fresh, attractive, brisk and assured of manner.

FLORENCE. Hello, Mother!
DAISY. Hello, Florence. You're home early.
FLORENCE. Just my usual time.
DAISY. Then I must be behind.
FLORENCE. I expect you are. It's nearly five o'clock.
DAISY. Ee, and I haven't got my housekeeping book balanced.
FLORENCE (*moving down R*) You're on the last minute with those accounts every Friday.
DAISY. I know, love. I keep putting off the final reckoning. What's six pounds seventeen and ninepence-ha'penny and four pounds nine and tenpence-ha'penny?
FLORENCE (*instantly, as she continues moving down R*) Eleven pounds seven and eightpence.
DAISY. You've got your father's head for sums.
FLORENCE. Have I? Thank you. (*She transfers her clutch bag and exercise books from the briefcase to the table down R*)
DAISY. It's still not right. Dash this weekly reckoning up! Florence, you wouldn't just run your eye over these figures for me, love, just to make sure they're okay?

FLORENCE (*taking her spectacles from her bag*) It's every week the same. (*She sits L of the table and runs her pencil up the row of figures*)

DAISY. I've simply got to make them all tally before your dad gets home. You know he likes everything to be just so.

FLORENCE (*adding up quickly*) Ten pounds one and threepence.

DAISY. That sum has an honest ring. (*She gives some coins to Florence*) When does school break up, love?

FLORENCE. For Easter? Next Wednesday. You've a deficit of twenty-six shillings and fivepence on paper.

DAISY. I can't have.

FLORENCE. I know—but you have.

DAISY. I wonder where it all goes! Florence, love, could you advance me a pound until after Dad's given me the housekeeping money? Just to keep his mind at rest.

(FLORENCE *takes a note out of her bag and hands it to Daisy*)

FLORENCE (*disapproving*) One pound.

DAISY. Ta, love. Don't be surprised if you get home one Friday and I've done a bunk.

FLORENCE (*returning the coins*) It's your own fault—you should put down on paper every . . .

DAISY (*cutting in*) I know—every item as I pay for it! That's what your dad keeps telling me. Well, the money's right, it was only the reckoning that was wrong.

FLORENCE (*returning the notebook and putting away her spectacles*) And that's still not right. You're six and fivepence out.

DAISY. So I am. Now suppose I'd paid the window-cleaner—which I haven't, because he hasn't been.

FLORENCE. Mother!

DAISY. There's nothing dishonest about it. It's just for your dad's peace of mind. (*She takes the notebook and begins to write in it*) Window-cleaner, eight-and-six. That takes me out of the red, and puts me a couple of bob to the good. Funny, but I can get away with that touch nearly every week. It seems to be his one blind spot.

FLORENCE. God help you if he ever finds out.

DAISY. God help him, poor chap, he has such faith in me. Is Arthur coming round tonight?

FLORENCE. I hope not. I've some markings to do. Three nights a week of Arthur is quite enough.

DAISY. Once you get married you'll have seven nights a week of him. And not just holding hands in the pictures either!

FLORENCE. That won't be for some time yet, I hope.

DAISY. You never know your luck.

(BETSY JANE, *a neighbourly slattern, enters by the back door. She is obviously in a hurry. The light starts to fade slowly as dusk falls*)

BETSY JANE. I say, Daisy!

DAISY. That you, Betsy Jane? (*She rises and moves up R*)

(BETSY JANE *enters the living-room. She sees Florence and her manner changes*)

BETSY JANE. Hello, Florence.

FLORENCE. Hello.

BETSY JANE (*looking round*) Your mother's got all her week-end cleaning and polishing done—just fancy!

DAISY (*laying the table with cutlery from the sideboard*) Aye, Rafe always likes to come home to everything spick and span of a Friday.

BETSY JANE. He would! But he wouldn't get it from me. (*She sniffs*) I see you're having herrings for tea.

DAISY (*setting the jam pot and spoon*) Yes, and they're lovely. Fancy a couple?

BETSY JANE. I wouldn't give a thank-you for all the herring in the North Sea. I'm more partial to sausages or black pudding. Something savoury like.

DAISY. Rafe has always liked fish of a Friday.

BETSY JANE. I suppose you others have got to like it.

FLORENCE. And why shouldn't we?

DAISY. Why—what's wrong with a good fresh herring?

BETSY JANE. You needn't get up in arms! I only thought it a bit High Church for a chap as were eddicated at Cotton Lane Baptists. 'Course, they do say they're very nutritious.

FLORENCE (*rising and moving up* C) Really! I'll go and change.

(*A buzzer sounds*)

Now don't get behind, Mother—that's the buzzer.

DAISY (*moving her bag to the sideboard*) No, I'd better not.

BETSY JANE. I'll be off in a minute, Florence. I just wanted a word in private with your mum.

(FLORENCE *exits up* C. BETSY JANE *cocks a snook*)

Eee, I thought she was never going.

DAISY. What's up, Betsy Jane?

BETSY JANE. Daisy, I'm in a right mess! Could you let me have five pounds?

DAISY. Five pounds! I'm sorry, but . . .

BETSY JANE. It's the flaming television fella. I'm behind with my payments, and he's just come to take it back if I don't pay five pounds off the arrears.

DAISY (*moving to the* L *armchair*) You don't mean to say he's in there now?

BETSY JANE. Aye, I left the front door on the latch and he caught me. And now he's got it all disconnected ready to take back unless I hand him over five pounds in ready cash.

DAISY (*sitting on the arm of the* L *armchair*) You couldn't have come at a worse time.

BETSY JANE. Yon chap will murder me if he gets home and finds the telly gone. He thinks I'm straight up with all my payments.

DAISY. I'm so sorry . . .

BETSY JANE. And think of the disgrace in front of all my neighbours if they see that fella carrying it out.

DAISY. I'm sorry, but . . .

BETSY JANE. I swear my oath I'll let you have it back by seven o'clock—as soon as he hands over his money.

DAISY. Rafe's got this obsession about keeping accounts straight. He likes to start every week afresh.

BETSY JANE. I wish I could start afresh.

DAISY. Would two pound ten see you through? (*She opens her bag*)

BETSY JANE. He won't budge under five pounds. I'm sure you could fiddle the other fifty bob one way or another.

DAISY. The other? I'll have to fiddle for the first. Is there nobody else you could ask?

BETSY JANE. Is there hell as like! They're all as badly off as me. Do try to wangle the five pounds.

DAISY. Look, it'll take me all my time to get you fifty bob.

BETSY JANE. Tell him you've paid some bill you haven't.

DAISY. I wouldn't want to tell a barefaced lie to Rafe.

BETSY JANE. Why not? Anyway, what right has he to interfere with your housekeeping? That's the wife's job.

DAISY. So long as all the bills are paid I'm happy running the house.

BETSY JANE. How can you say you're happy? And how do you run the house? Money runs the house, and that jumped-up husband of your's handles it all.

DAISY. Now don't you be so cheeky in my home. Rafe has never seen me short of money and we don't owe a halfpenny. How many wives on this estate could say that?

BETSY JANE. Well, we owe everybody and I'm always short of money, and the television chap's in possession at the moment, but I've still got something you haven't got.

DAISY. What's that? What've you got I haven't?

BETSY JANE. A wife's pride! Aye, and independence.

DAISY (*rising*) How dare you say I've no pride!

BETSY JANE. I dare because it's true. They all say it, all your neighbours. They're always talking about you and him and his domineering ways.

DAISY (*shocked*) You mean my neighbours talk about me behind my back?

BETSY JANE. Yes, they do.

DAISY. I don't believe it.

(WILFRED CROMPTON *enters by the back door. He is eighteen but looks younger. He is wearing a factory mechanic's blue bib overalls and a cap.*

*During the following speech he removes these and hangs them on a peg on
the door)*

BETSY JANE. Don't you! Why, Mrs Clegg was only saying the
other day what she'd do if a man dared attempt to run her side of
the home. He might manage to have everything paid up, he might
manage to keep the house in order, but in doing it he's sucked all
the pride out of you. You talk about not telling him a lie—why, all
your life is a flaming lie, if you ask me. How can a man run a home?
That's the woman's job, always has been. A man has no right to
attempt it. It's not natural.

(WILFRED *enters the living-room*)

WILFRED. What's not natural?
BETSY JANE (*with a snort*) Oh, go to hell!

(BETSY JANE *exits to the kitchen with a look at Daisy, then goes out
by the back door*)

WILFRED. What the heck's up with her? (*Noticing that Daisy is
upset*) Has something upset you, Mum?
DAISY. Listen, Wilf, would you say I had no pride?
WILFRED. No pride—you, Mum! Who dare say that? (*He kisses her*)
You've pride in everything you touch.
DAISY (*unconvinced*) Bless you, lad. Call her back.

(WILFRED *puts his jacket on the L armchair, hurries to the back door
and whistles*)

WILFRED. Hi! Betsy Jane! Come back, my mum wants you.

(DAISY *goes into the kitchen and then to the back door*)

What was up with her?
DAISY. Could you let me have five pounds, love, out of your
wages?
WILFRED. Five pound! Aye, I expect I could at a pinch. (*He
takes out his wage packet and extracts notes*) It might throw me a bit
short for when I'm paying over to Dad.
DAISY. I'll get a couple of pounds off your Harold for you—just
to tide you over.
WILFRED. Good. I say, you're not lending it to Betsy Jane, are
you?
DAISY. It's all right. She's got some trouble. You won't let your
father know?
WILFRED. What he doesn't know won't keep him awake. But I
don't trust her.

(BETSY JANE, *shamefaced, enters the back door.* WILFRED *picks up the
cat from outside and takes it into the living-room*)

BETSY JANE. What is it, Daisy?

DAISY. Here, your five pound. I got it off our Wilf. Get in home before it's too late.

BETSY JANE. Ee, no thanks—I can't take it—not after what I said to you.

DAISY. Let's say no more about it.

BETSY JANE. (*briskly*) Ta then. You're a good neighbour, Daisy. It's terrible when you've nobody to turn to. I'll let you have it back the minute yon chap hands over his money to me. He's never later than seven. I hope I can do as much for you one day. (*She turns to go*)

DAISY. Hey, I say . . .

(BETSY JANE *turns back*)

Do they—do my neighbours really talk about me in that way?

BETSY JANE. Eh? Now don't take what I said to heart.

DAISY. I'm asking you.

BETSY JANE. Not really. I think it's only jealousy. They all envy you your nice home. You know how they are—don't like to see anybody better off than themselves. Try to forget what I said.

(BETSY JANE *hurries off.* DAISY *wipes her eye and returns slowly to the living-room*)

WILFRED. Has anything upset you, Mum?

DAISY. I've just heard a bit of truth, love—it can be upsetting.

WILFRED. Take no notice of what she says.

DAISY. I'll go and wash me.

WILFRED. And I'll grab the sink while I've a chance.

(DAISY *exits up* C. WILFRED *takes the cat to the kitchen, then enters the scullery, switching on the light.* HAROLD CROMPTON *enters through the back door, whistling. He is in his twenties and has a dry, comical air. He works in a spinning mill and wears corduroy trousers and bicycle clips, a cardigan, cap and scarf*)

Howgo, Harold!

HAROLD. Howgo, squire!

(WILFRED *throws a towel over his shoulders and washes his face and hands at the sink.* HAROLD *hangs up his scarf and takes off his clips*)

WILFRED. You can come and have a sluice here in a minute.

HAROLD (*taking the towel and wiping his hands*) I don't need to wash me. We're working on Egyptians—beautiful cotton—spins like silk. How come our Hilda's not home with you?

WILFRED. They were having a bit of a do over in the weaving shed. Some chap getting wed.

HAROLD. There's one born every minute. (*He goes into the living-room and sits on the* L *armchair with his feet up*)

WILFRED. No, there's always a big rush before Easter to save the income tax.

HAROLD. I'll bet that's not the only reason they're rushing. (*He takes out a cigarette and lights it*)

WILFRED (*moving into the living-room*) Why—what other?

HAROLD (*throwing the towel at Wilfred*) Skip it, son.

WILFRED. Hey, you mucky beggar, look what a mess you've made of this towel.

HAROLD. Don't worry. I'll send you to the launderette with it in the morning.

(FLORENCE *enters up* C, *switching on the pendant and desk lamp by the switch* L *of the door*)

WILFRED. Some hopes you've got! Hello, Flo.

FLORENCE. Hello, love.

HAROLD (*in a posh voice*) Hello, Flo. Where's Mum?

WILFRED. Having a wash in t'bathroom. (*Drying his face and buttoning his cuffs*) Hi, that reminds me, you've got to give me a couple of quid.

HAROLD. I have! What for?

WILFRED. Mum'll tell you. She's been lending money.

HAROLD. Keep me out of your mother's troubles. I'm very short myself this week—I've backed a few losers.

FLORENCE (*moving to the fire down* C, *pushing Harold's feet aside to get the coal glove*) Can't you keep your big feet out of the way?

HAROLD. Do you call twelve-and-a-halfs big? The old man takes fifteens.

FLORENCE (*putting coal on the fire*) If you mean your father say your father.

HAROLD. I don't. I mean the old man, old Crompton. Ever heard of him?

FLORENCE. I'd like to see you if he comes in and catches you in his chair—and stinking the room with your fags.

HAROLD. That little word "if".

WILFRED (*putting on his jacket and combing his hair*) Better get the Airwick spray out, mate, or he'll smell you've been smoking.

HAROLD. I don't care what he smells. Let him come to me if he has any complaints—and I'll tell him where he gets off.

(FLORENCE *goes to the sideboard and then sits the napkins on the table*)

WILFRED. Don't forget tonight's his monthly union meeting. So don't you set him off.

(WILFRED *exits to the kitchen with the towel*)

HAROLD. I should worry! No wonder the last union secretary ended up where he did.

(HILDA CROMPTON *runs in from the front door and enters the sitting-room. She is aged nineteen and is a weaver at the mills. She is fresh and gay.*

She carries a shoulder-bag and "Weekend" magazine, and wears a bright raincoat)

HILDA. Oh, I have had a good time! *(She moves to the piano)*
HAROLD. Be careful your dad doesn't hear you.
HILDA. He's not home yet?
FLORENCE. Of course not. It's not Dad's time yet.
HILDA. Thank heaven. Where's Mum? *(She takes off her raincoat and leaves her things on the piano-stool)*
HAROLD *(cutting in)* She's run off with Co-op coal chap—they've made off for Blackpool with his week's takings.

(HILDA pushes Harold's cap over his eyes. HAROLD takes it off. DAISY enters, smiling)

DAISY. Here I am, love. Ee, you do look bonny. *(She hugs Hilda)*
HILDA. Ee, we have had a good time, Mum! We've had a lovely footing.
DAISY. Yes, love—you look it. Straighten your hair.
FLORENCE. You've had a what?
HAROLD *(mimicking)* A party—where they all foot their share.
HILDA *(looking in the mirror L)* Yes—our mechanic's getting married tomorrow, so all the weavers in our shed pooled seven-and-six apiece for a cheese and wine party. It was lovely.
DAISY. Ee, we only had cider and sausage rolls in my time.
HAROLD. Aye, things were tight during the Boer War.
HILDA. Smell my breath, Mum! I'd about three glassfulls of port.
HAROLD. I can smell it from here. Springtime orgies in the weaving shed.

(WILFRED enters from the kitchen)

HILDA. Wilf, love, could you hear us singing hymns after?
FLORENCE. Hymns on top of that lot!

(FLORENCE snorts and exits to the kitchen)

WILFRED. Aye, we could even hear you in the mechanics' shop with the lathe going. *(He plays the piano)*

(HILDA, DAISY and WILFRED sing. As they do so, HILDA picks up her things and Harold's cap. She puts her bag and the cap on the piano, hangs her mac up in the hall, and returns with the magazine. DAISY sets the cruet and sugar on the table)

HILDA
DAISY   } *(singing)* { Follow, follow, I will follow Jesus.
WILFRED   { Anywhere, everywhere, I will follow on.
HAROLD. Funny choice for a party piece.
HILDA
DAISY   } *(singing)* Follow, follow, I will follow Jesus.
WILFRED

HAROLD. Hey, Daisy, cut out the yodelling. I'm starving.
HILDA ⎫
DAISY ⎬ (*singing*)   Anywhere He leads, I will follow on.
WILFRED ⎭

(*They stop singing, and* WILFRED *turns and whispers to Daisy*)

DAISY. Harold love, give our Wilf two pounds for me.
HAROLD. What for?
DAISY. I'll let you have it back later when Betsy Jane settles up with me.
HAROLD. You been lending that one money? You want your head examining.

(HILDA *moves to the desk*)

WILFRED. Come on, hand over . . .
DAISY. It's for my sake.
HAROLD. All right—I'll do it for you, Mum.

(HAROLD *reluctantly gives Wilfred two pounds.* HILDA *looks at the letters on the desk.* DAISY *watches her*)

(*To Wilfred*) Don't forget I want it back, mate.
WILFRED. I don't owe it to you.
DAISY. I'm afraid there's no letter for you, love.
HILDA. It's all right.
HAROLD. He's forgot you, girl.
HILDA. Who?
HAROLD. As if you didn't know! Start frying them herrings, Mum.

(FLORENCE *enters with two plates of bread-and-butter.* HAROLD *rises, takes a slice, and sits again putting his feet up.* HILDA *sits on the pouffe down* L. FLORENCE *puts the plates on the table*)

HILDA. Who said herrings? Don't say we're having herrings!
WILFRED. I thought you liked them.
HAROLD. So did I!
HILDA. Well, I've gone off 'em.
DAISY. That's funny.
HILDA. What's funny?
DAISY. Nothing.
HAROLD. She is getting above herself.
DAISY. Your dad asked for them special.

(DAISY *looks at Hilda and exits to the kitchen*)

FLORENCE (*drawing the curtains* R) And what's wrong with herrings?
HILDA. I don't know—I've just gone off 'em.
HAROLD. Well, they don't go with port wine.
DAISY (*off*) Hey—Wilf! Come and get your cat from under my feet, and put him outside.

WILFRED (*moving up* L) Coming, Mum. They say they're brain food, you know.

(WILFRED *exits to the kitchen*)

HAROLD. Then you'd better eat our Hilda's.

HILDA. The thought of them puts me off.

HAROLD (*in a lady-like voice*) Do they repeat on you, deah? (*He belches*)

HILDA (*rising; miserably*) I don't know how it is—but I've only to smell 'em these days . . . (*She hits Harold's feet, crosses to the standard lamp up* R, *switches it on, then sits on the sofa* R *and reads her magazine*)

HAROLD. I've noticed you're getting a bit fussy. Mind you, I wouldn't object to fillet steak for a change, and a bottle of vintage Beaujolais. But what puts me off is waiting. Why do we always have to wait for him for our tea? Who does he think he is?

(WILFRED *enters the scullery from the kitchen with the cat and a saucer and exits through the back door*)

FLORENCE (*moving to Harold*) What else would we do?

HAROLD (*rising*) What I say is let's all sit down and start tea right now. First come first served. Come on—who's game?

FLORENCE. I'd like to see the day when you dare.

(WILFRED *rushes in through the back door and round into the living-room*)

HAROLD (*sitting again*) Well, if he says anything to me I'll send him about his business. I've stood just about enough of his old guff. After all, we are living in a democracy, you know.

WILFRED (*tapping Harold's houlder*) He's just turned the top of the crescent.

HAROLD (*casually*) Who do you think you're kidding? (*With alarm*) He's not, has he? (*He rises*) The old man . . . ?

(FLORENCE *exits to the kitchen.* DAISY *enters with tartare sauce and moves to the table*)

(*Agitatedly flapping a paper about*) Here, help me. Waft this smoke about. Come on, quick. (*He stubs out his cigarette in the coal scuttle*) Get going! Turn the telly on, it'll take his mind off things.

(DAISY, *with calm assurance, tidies the easy chair.* WILFRED *turns on the television*)

Hey, Mum, can you smell the smoke?

DAISY. I'll start putting the herrings on, that'll kill it.

(*The television sound and light flicker come on.* DAISY *exits to the kitchen, switching on the light. After finally wafting the smoke away,* HAROLD *joins* WILFRED *watching the television, which becomes noisy.* RAFE CROMPTON *enters from the front door. He has a solid, fatherly look and is a man very much himself. He is a cotton-mill worker, aged about fifty. There is nothing grim or stern about him—he is just quietly sure of himself. He hangs up his cap in the hall then enters the living-room. He has with him his thermos, lunch-box, and copy of the evening paper. He walks quietly across to the television set and switches it off)*

RAFE. I don't think we need that one. . . . Listen to that silence. (*He listens*) Just feel how soothing a bit of quiet is. (*He throws the newspaper into his armchair*)

WILFRED. I thought it would liven things up, Dad.

HAROLD. Aye, that's right.

RAFE. I don't need livening up. You two might, but I don't. What I need after my day's work is a bit of peace.

(DAISY *enters, moves to Rafe, kisses him, then takes his thermos and lunch-box*)

DAISY. Hello, Dad.

RAFE. 'Mother.

DAISY. Had a hard day?

RAFE (*taking off his jacket*) The work in the engine shed is not nearly as hard as it used to be, but somehow it's more wearing.

DAISY (*putting Rafe's jacket on the back of his chair*) I expect it begins to tell on you by the week-end. Tea'll be ready soon.

RAFE. Good.

(DAISY *exits into the kitchen*)

(*Sniffing*) Have you been smoking those fags again?

(HAROLD *shakes his head, then coughs*)

Just before your meal. (*Moving* R) When will you learn some sense? (*He opens the window. To Hilda*) Hello, love.

HILDA. Hello, Dad.

RAFE (*sniffing and looking at Hilda*) Funny, I thought I could smell drink.

HILDA. We had a party in the mill, and I had some port wine.

RAFE. You know what they say—wine is a turncoat—starts off as a friend and then turns into an enemy.

HILDA. I didn't reach that stage.

RAFE (*reading a headline over Hilda's shoulder*) "What happened after the dance. Teenagers' night of sex and drugs." Do you have to waste your money on such trash?

HILDA. I didn't buy it. Betty Partington gave it me.

RAFE. But why fill your mind with that muck?

HILDA. It's the truth, after all.

WILFRED. Aye, there's that to it, Dad.

HAROLD. You've got to face facts in this life.

RAFE (*moving to the piano*) Nay, it might be news, but it's never truth. (*He picks up the family Bible*) You may question every fact in this holy book—but who dare say every word isn't God's truth!

(FLORENCE *enters carrying Rafe's slippers*)

FLORENCE. Here are your slippers, Dad.

RAFE. Thank you, Florence. (*He takes a book from the number on the piano—"A Book of Sixteenth Century Verse"*) Truth is a spiritual thing, it survives the centuries, whereas the chap who wrote that filth had only one thing in mind—to sell his rotten magazines. It's their trade, see. Now listen to this—this is what I call truth.

(FLORENCE *sits on the piano stool to listen.* HAROLD *mimes the words in time with Rafe*)

"When I do count the clock that tells the time,
And see the brave day sunk in hideous night;
When I behold the violet past prime,
And sable curls all silvered o'er with white;
When lofty trees I see barren of leaves,
Which . . ." (*He raises his head and loses the place*)

HAROLD. "Which erst from heat did canopy the herd!"

RAFE. Thank you very much. (*He replaces the book and puts his slippers on*) I only hope they take me away in my wooden box when I fail to be stirred by such beauty.

HILDA. Folk would think you were daft if you walked about with a book of poetry under your arm.

RAFE. Who cares what folk think? I don't. If most folk were to know what other folk thought about them, they'd drop dead with shock.

HAROLD. Some would—that's for sure!

FLORENCE (*moving to her handbag and taking out money*) Dad, before I forget, I went to the bank in the lunch hour. Here's my week's money. Will you take it now?

RAFE. I might as well get it over with. Just a tick. I've a good idea what a lot of folk think I am.

HAROLD. You can't stop them from thinking.

(HILDA *rises.* WILFRED, HAROLD *and* HILDA *begin to take money from their wage packets with varying reluctance and secrecy, moving up* C. RAFE *crosses to the desk, takes a key from his pocket, opens the desk and takes out a small security box which he unlocks and opens. He takes a wage packet from his pocket, picks up a long paper-knife, slits the packet open, and puts some notes in the security box. He then takes Florence's money*)

RAFE. Thank you.

(HILDA *puts a five-pound note on the desk in an offhand manner and returns to the sofa*)

Thank you.

(FLORENCE *picks up Rafe's boots and exits into the kitchen*)

WILFRED. Here's my bagging money, Dad. (*He hands over five pounds*) You'll find that right, I think.

(DAISY *enters with a butter-dish which she places on the table. She then returns to the kitchen*)

RAFE (*in the manner of a bank clerk, with no interest in money as such*) Thank you.

(WILFRED *moves away up* C)

HAROLD (*hurriedly*) Here y'are, Dad . . .
RAFE. Thank you . . .

(RAFE *never counts, but he knows*)

Hey, what's this?
HAROLD. Eh? Eh—what's what?
RAFE. You're a pound short.
HAROLD (*too quickly*) Eh? Oh, sorry, Dad—sorry. (*He takes a pound note out of his back pocket*)
RAFE. I'm not one of them, lad. (*Calling*) Mother!
HAROLD. One of what?
RAFE. You know—one of them you seem to take me for! (*He takes the note*)

(DAISY *enters from the kitchen with a trolley loaded with the tea things*)

DAISY. Tea's ready, everybody. Yes, Dad?

(HAROLD *takes his plate off the trolley and sits at the table, on the chair up* R. WILFRED *helps* DAISY *to lay the rest of the plates*)

RAFE. How did you manage this week with your housekeeping money, Mother?
DAISY. Oh, I've a bit left. You'll see it there.
RAFE (*putting the housekeeping money out on the desk and locking the cash-box*) Did it work out right on paper—I mean in figures?
DAISY. I think so—near enough.
RAFE. Just let me see it, Mother—just to cast an eye over it.
DAISY. It's there, in my bag. (*She indicates the sideboard*)

(RAFE *opens Daisy's bag and takes out the notebook*)

RAFE. By gum, the price of meat these days—no wonder yon butcher drives round in a Jag. I see the window-cleaner was round again. Fair enough, Mother, you're even a shilling or two to the good according to my reckoning. I'll make a chartered accountant of you yet. (*He puts the housekeeping money in the book and locks the desk*)
DAISY. Don't aim too high, Dad.
RAFE. You're doing very well, Mother. At times you astonish me.
DAISY. At times I astonish myself.

RAFE (*taking off his collar and tie and crossing to the table*) But always take care of the pence . . .

HAROLD (*aside*) And he'll take care of the pounds!

(*We are never sure whether* RAFE *hears*)

RAFE (*holding out the book and money*) Here's your next week's money, Mother. Don't stint yourself, and let me know if you're running short.

DAISY. Will you put it down by my handbag. Come on to your tea, now.

RAFE (*putting the money, book, collar and tie on the sideboard*) You should always check it. Even from me! I'll go and rinse my hands first. Money can be a good servant—but a very poor master. So always have it right.

(RAFE *exits up* C. *As soon as the door is closed,* HAROLD *lets out a raspberry*)

DAISY. Harold! (*She taps him on the shoulder as she goes to the sideboard to sort out the money*)

(FLORENCE *enters from the kitchen with the teapot. She switches off the kitchen light and takes the pot to the trolley*)

WILFRED. You didn't get away with it, did you?

HAROLD. Away with what? Oh, you mean the quid short? It was a genuine mistake.

WILFRED. You can't get past him.

HAROLD. Him—I could get that feller down with chicken feed. Hey, Daisy, let's get cracking—I'm famished.

FLORENCE. You'll wait until your father takes his place.

HAROLD. Who says I will? (*He grabs a slice of bread and butter*)

FLORENCE (*slapping his hand*) You greedy beggar. Don't let Dad catch you slancing.

HAROLD. I don't care what he catches me at!

DAISY. Come on, Hilda love, sit in.

HILDA. I'm not that hungry.

HAROLD. No, but we are. Come on.

(HILDA *hesitates, then slowly walks to her place, which is the down-stage* L *chair.* WILFRED *moves to his place, below Harold.* DAISY *regards the table, which is now laid*)

DAISY. Oh, Florence, before I forget I must give you that pound you lent me.

WILFRED. You're doing a lot of money juggling, Mum.

DAISY. Ssh! (*She takes a note and hands it to Florence*) Ta very much.

FLORENCE. Oh, thanks, Mother. (*She takes the note*)

(RAFE *enters, spotting* DAISY's *guilty movement. They all sit down to tea:* RAFE *above the table,* FLORENCE *to* L *of him,* DAISY *below Wilfred*)

RAFE. What was that, Mother?

DAISY. A little something I borrowed off our Florence.

RAFE (*quoting*) "Neither a borrower nor a lender be . . ."

HAROLD. Hey, Wilf, pass the tartare sauce.

WILFRED. The what?

FLORENCE. Sauce tartare. (*She picks it up*) Here you are.

HAROLD. Ta ta. "For loan oft loses both itself and friend." Do you fancy some, Dad?

RAFE. I prefer the natural taste of the herring.

HAROLD. I find this sauce quite piquant. How much a jar is it, Mum?

DAISY. I don't know—oh, one-and-ninepence. I knew there was something I didn't write down. (*She starts to rise, then sits*) I'll do it later.

(RAFE *looks at her*)

HAROLD. What about you, Florence?

FLORENCE. I'll give it a miss. These taste lovely as they are.

HILDA. I say, Mum, I really don't fancy my herring—if you don't mind.

DAISY. No, of course not, love! What would you like instead? I've got some nice fresh eggs.

HAROLD. Aye, with some streaky rashers.

HILDA. No, just an egg.

HAROLD. Sunny side up?

HILDA. Done on both sides. But wait till you're finished, Mum.

DAISY. It's all right, love—won't take me a minute. (*Rising*) You must be ready for it after a day's work. . . .

(*They think they have got away with it, but* RAFE *quietly beckons* DAISY *to sit*)

RAFE. Hold on a minute, Mother. (*To Hilda*) Is there something wrong with your herring?

HILDA. No, nothing wrong with it—only I don't feel like it.

RAFE. That's a lovely fresh herring, it's been done in best butter, and yet you have the nerve to sit there and say you don't feel like it.

HILDA. What else can I say if I don't?

RAFE. You can eat it and say nothing.

HAROLD. Well, that's asking a bit much, Dad!

HILDA. I'll just go and fry myself an egg, Mum!

RAFE. No, you won't.

HILDA. Why not?

RAFE. Because this is a home, not a cafeteria.

HILDA. I'm entitled to some choice over what I have for my tea—I'm bringing my share of money into the home.

RAFE. You don't think I thought less of you over all the years you never brought in a ha'penny? I'd as soon see the smiling face you had in them days than you were bringing twenty pounds a week home today.

WILFRED. Here, Dad, to save any bother, I'll eat our Hilda's herring.

RAFE. You'll do nothing of the sort. You get on with your own tea.

DAISY (*not put out*) Dad—it wouldn't take a second to fry an egg.

RAFE. There's no fried eggs coming on the scene.

HILDA. Then there's no point in my waiting here. (*Rising*) Excuse me, everybody—I'll just go upstairs . . .

RAFE (*quietly*) No you won't. Sit down.

HILDA. What?

RAFE. I said sit down.

(HILDA *is undecided.* DAISY *gives her a pleading look*)

Pigs leave their troughs when it suits—but not civilized human beings.

(WILFRED *gives Hilda a look of sympathetic support,* FLORENCE *gives her a reproving glance.* HAROLD *continues to eat with an air of detached interest about the outcome.* DAISY *does not want trouble, but gives Hilda a comforting, motherly look*)

DAISY. Dad—I'll just . . .

(RAFE *remains oddly above it all, continuing to eat naturally as he talks.* HILDA *catches Daisy's look and sits down, but away from the table*)

RAFE. No, you won't, Mother. They were never spoilt when young—it 'ud be a pity to start now. One day, young woman, you may realize what words like home and family mean. A man and woman marry, they have children, feed and tend 'em, work for 'em, guide, aye, an' love 'em.

HILDA. Just as they ought.

RAFE. Aye, I agree—as they ought. Over the years they try to make a home for those children, not just a furnished place to live in, but a home, mark you, with some culture. But do those children thank you? Well, perhaps some do—mostly they don't. They take you an' your home for granted. Well, there's nobody taking me for granted.

HILDA. I don't see why I should eat that herring if I don't want it . . .

RAFE (*detached*) Then I'll tell you one reason why—as comes to mind at the moment. Pass me the bread, Florence, please. Have you ever heard of the Hunger Marchers?

(FLORENCE *passes the bread.* RAFE *takes a piece*)

HILDA. Yes, folk out in foreign countries.

RAFE. I mean folk in this country. Thank you, Florence. (*Eating as he talks*) Something you never realized.

WILFRED. Must have been in the old days, Dad.

RAFE. It was when your brother Harold here was a babe in arms and your mother was six months carrying our Florence. That's when it was. I was out of work at the time. One day we set off to Queen's Park to have a picnic. We'd some flour cakes and a bottle of cold tea. On Chorley Old Road we suddenly came on the Hunger Marchers marching along.

WILFRED. Who were they, Dad, and where were they off to?

RAFE. They were men down from the Clydeside. Men who'd been out of work for years, and had seen their wives and families go hungry. A band of them got together to walk the four hundred miles' stretch to the Houses of Parliament. Mother, do you remember their feet, all sore and bandaged up?

DAISY. Yes—and I remember their faces. They were singing, weren't they?

RAFE. Nay, not singing, Mother, whistling. I don't think they had the strength to sing, but by heck they could whistle.

DAISY. Yes, they were whistling "Loch Lomond".

RAFE (to Hilda) We were standing there as they went by. I can hear 'em this minute. Your mother nudged me as one weary-looking chap came up. The next thing she'd taken the flour cakes from under my arm and handed them to him. And on they went. That didn't happen in foreign countries; it happened here. And once you've lived through it you don't forget it.

HILDA. But it can't happen these days.

HAROLD. Them times are gone for ever.

RAFE. That's what I thought before it happened to me.

HAROLD. You can't have another depression—they've got economic planning that makes it impossible.

RAFE. If the Government suddenly decided there were too many cars on the road—and put a curb on production—there could be thousands out of work next month.

FLORENCE. What happened to you, Dad?

RAFE (eating as he talks) At the mill where I'd worked from a boy they'd made me engine tenter over Nellie, as we called her. I thought I'd a job for life, looking after the engine. Till one clever official up in London decided it would pay them to close down a few hundred mills and have the machinery broken up. Economic Planning, see.

WILFRED. Why, Dad?

RAFE. Hitler were paying a big price for scrap iron, needed all he could get. It was a chance not to be missed. So they gave us all a week's notice, shut the mill down one Friday, and on the Monday after they had scrap men in, smashing the machinery up.

FLORENCE. Was it hard to get work in those times?

RAFE. It wasn't all that easy—with well over half the country out of work, searching for jobs. It took me eighteen months. Hardly a week went by but they'll pull some poor chap out of yon canal down the road. (He thumbs over his shoulder)

DAISY. Aye, and many a poor woman too.

WILFRED. And did they smash her up—your engine, Nellie?

RAFE. What else? I told you Hitler urgently needed all the scrap-iron he could lay hands on for making guns and shells and bombs. Mind you, we got most of it back around nineteen-forty.

HILDA. Hitler! Why bring him up? That's all a thing of the past—it's another world.

RAFE. It might be to you—but it's not to me.

HILDA. Well, I still don't see what all this has got to do with a herring.

(WILFRED *nods in agreement.* RAFE *silences him with a look*)

RAFE. Look at your mother—in those days she was a young woman, and a bonny woman, not much older than you are now—and she hadn't had a decent meal in months. She would have given thanks to God for that good wholesome food on your plate. But she was lucky to get a bit of bread and dripping, or the odd slice of potted meat. (*With a rising outburst*) So I won't have you sit there in front of me and see you make little of good food! Because you're making little of the life we've had to live! And millions like us.

DAISY. Dad—calm yourself.

RAFE. I can't stand the way young people are today—all for themselves, and all for the present, as though the past didn't exist.

DAISY (*always achieving a balance of sympathy*) More tea, Dad?

RAFE. No, thank you, Mother—not just now. (*Rising*) But there is one thing you can do for me—have that herring of our Hilda's safely put on one side—and you serve it to her, and nothing else, at every meal—until she eats it! I'm having no more sloppy living under my roof. (*He picks up his jacket*)

HILDA. I won't eat it . . .

RAFE We'll see—because you'll eat nothing at my table until you have. (*He picks up his collar and tie*)

HILDA. I won't touch it! Not if it's there till Kingdom come!

RAFE. Right, we'll see the outcome. I'll go and get ready for my union meeting. If you get the better of me you'll be the first in this house who has. Mother, I'm relying on you over that herring.

DAISY. I'll get it out of the way at once, Dad.

(RAFE *exits up* C. DAISY *has seen quarrels come and go and doesn't take them too seriously. She gives Hilda a pat, then exits to the kitchen with the herring*)

HAROLD (*to Hilda*) Don't worry—they'll be comin' to take him away in the yellow cab very soon, the way he's going on. He's obsessed.

FLORENCE (*angrily*) Don't you be so stupid!

HAROLD. What—a scene like that all over a herring? He must be mad.

FLORENCE. It's not over a herring—it's over a principle. You've got to have some order in a home.

HILDA. Oh, shut up, our Florence! You're as bad as him.

WILFRED. Now then, now then, let's not row . . .

FLORENCE. If she had eaten her tea there'd have been no row. She's full of likes and dislikes lately.

HAROLD. She's been on the port wine, hasn't she!

(*There is a knock on the front door*)

Sumdy at door, Wilf!

FLORENCE (*rising*) It's all right—I'll go. You know Dad detests anybody fussing over their food—not eating what's put in front of them. With half the world starving.

(FLORENCE *exits up* C *to the front door*)

HILDA. Dad—Dad—Dad—you'd think he was the only one in the house!

WILFRED (*going to Hilda and putting his arm round her*) Take no notice, love.

HAROLD. I'll lay you two-to-one you'll eat that herring.

HILDA. I will hell as like!

HAROLD. I bet you.

HILDA. You're on.

HAROLD. Right, in dollars.

(DAISY *enters from the kitchen*)

DAISY. Don't worry, love, I'll get you something nice later.

HILDA. I'm sorry, Mum, for causing such a rumpus.

DAISY. We'll get over it, love.

HAROLD. If you meet me at Harry Wong's new Chinese restaurant at ten-thirty after the dogs, I'll buy you a chop suey butty. (*He makes a jam sandwich*)

(HILDA *rises and takes her handkerchief from her bag*)

WILFRED. You'll be on the borrow again if I know you—but don't come to me.

HAROLD. Don't you forget to collect my two pound.

(FLORENCE *enters carrying an expensively boxed parcel*)

FLORENCE. There's a parcel arrived for Dad, Mum.

(FLORENCE *puts the box on the table and helps* DAISY *to clear*)

DAISY. That's unusual—I wonder what it can be?

WILFRED (*reading the label*) Horsfall and Trott, Beespoke Tailors.

HAROLD (*rising and moving* C) Bespoke! Made to measure. I'll bet it's a fancy weskit for the engine tenters' ball. (*He. does a dance step, picks up Rafe's paper, and sits down* L)

WILFRED. I can't think what it can be!

Daisy. Neither can I.

Harold. The mysterious Mr Crompton—never lets his right hand know what his left hand is doing.

Wilfred. Listen for him coming downstairs, Mum. (*He takes out a bill*) It's an overcoat. "R. Crompton, Esq. One overcoat. Thirty-two guineas. Received with thanks."

Harold. Thirty-three pounds twelve for an overcoat! It can't be . . .

Wilfred. It is! look . . .

Harold. They must have seen him coming.

Daisy. If your father comes in and catches you prying into his business, I'll feel sorry for you.

Wilfred. For thirty-two guineas from Burton's I could have got him a lovely worsted made-to-measure suit, a new spring overcoat, and have enough left over for a pair of Chelsea boots.

Harold. You know what I think—as a lad he musta gone round starved to death with the cold—never knew what it was to have an overcoat—an' now he's trying to make it up to himself.

Florence (*putting the napkins away*) You've got a bit more understanding than I thought you had.

Wilfred. Get off—the way Dad talks of the Cromptons anybody would think they were the lords of creation.

Harold. Your father's come up in the world since he had us.

Hilda. I think it would have become him better to have paid a bit less, and bought a new coat for Mum.

Daisy. Your dad hasn't had a new overcoat for years. (*She pushes the trolley to the kitchen*)

Wilfred. And I'm not expecting he'll want another. Paying that price.

Daisy. I don't need a coat. Anyway, I could have one tomorrow if I asked him. (*She pushes the trolley inside the kitchen and returns*)

Hilda. You shouldn't have to ask him, Mum.

Florence (*putting the cruet, etc., away and using the crumb-tray from the sideboard*) Will you stop causing trouble. You know Dad would give Mother anything . . .

Harold. It he'd a couple of gumboils he wouldn't give you one.

Hilda. Why should he have all the say?

Daisy. Your dad would lay his life down for me.

Harold. It's not the same thing.

Daisy. Wilf, love, hurry up, he's coming.

(Wilfred *replaces the bill.* Rafe *enters. He is dressed to go to his union meeting and now wears shoes*)

Wilfred. Dad, there's a parcel for you.

Harold. It's from Horsfall and Trott's.

Rafe (*casually*) Oh aye, then it'll be an overcoat I ordered some time back. Will you take it upstairs for me, Florence?

Daisy. But aren't you going to try it on?

Rafe. I had two fittings, so it should be all right.

Florence. Go on, Dad, let's see you in it. (*She replaces the crumb-tray on the sideboard, puts the tablecloth in a drawer, and lays a runner and bowls of flowers on the table*)

Daisy. I should think so!

Harold. It might not fit right, you know. (*Sotto voce*) You can't trust these cheap tailors.

Wilfred (*crossing to the table* L *and taking a pair of scissors from the workbox on it*) Here you are, here's the scissors, Dad.

(Hilda *turns away*)

Rafe (*undoing the parcel*) Knots were made to be unfastened. It only needs patience. There we are.

Daisy. I'd like to see how it looks.

(Rafe *pockets the bill, unfastens the string, opens the box and removes the tissue paper.* Daisy *picks up the overcoat*)

That's a good cloth. It is for sure.

Florence (*moving* R *of Rafe*) Let me, Dad. (*She rubs her face against the cloth*) It's so soft and warm. Come on. (*She helps Rafe to put the coat on*)

(Rafe *stands* c)

Wilfred (*moving* L *of Rafe*) Silk-lined, Dad. Hand-stitched! And look, Harold, taped seams!

(Florence *and* Wilfred *pick fluff off the coat*)

Harold (*aside*) Aye, one sneeze and he's naked.

Rafe. No fussing, now. Anybody'ud think you'd never seen a new topcoat.

Harold (*aside*) We haven't—not one as cost that much.

Daisy (*rolling up the string*) That looks grand, Dad.

Wilfred. It's a good fit, eh, Harold?

Harold. Aye. (*Aside*) It fits where it touches.

Rafe. It's none too bad for these days.

Florence. Oh, it's lovely, Dad. You look so distinguished.

Rafe. I had a job to get the cloth. If you want the best you've got to pay for it. But it lasts that much longer.

(*There is a knock on the front door*)

Harold. Wilf, somebody at door!

(Wilfred *starts for the door.* Hilda *rises and looks through the window*)

Hilda. Oh, it's Arthur—shall I go, Florence.

Florence. You might as well.

(Hilda *exits* c *to the front door*)

He told me he was working overtime. I can't think what he wants
coming around here on a Friday.

HAROLD. I can't think what he wants coming round here at all.

DAISY. Show a bit more relish. He is your intended.

(RAFE *takes off the overcoat and moves* LC. FLORENCE *folds the coat*)

HILDA (*off*) Arthur, what a nice surprise.

(FLORENCE *moves* LC)

ARTHUR (*off*) Hello, Hilda.

(ARTHUR *enters with* HILDA *up* C. *He is a sheet metal worker, a quiet,
likeable chap of thirty, wearing overalls. He and* FLORENCE *look at each
other.* HILDA *moves to the sofa* R *and sits.* WILFRED *stands by the piano*)

Oh, hullo, Mr Crompton.

RAFE. Good evening, Arthur.

DAISY (*moving* R *of Arthur*) Well, how nice to see you, Arthur.

HAROLD ⎫
WILFRED ⎭ (*together*) Howgo, Arthur.

ARTHUR. Hullo, Mother. I'm sorry to butt in like this . . .

RAFE (*moving to the desk*) Never be ashamed of a bit of honest
dirt, lad, there's not enough of it knocking about these days. (*He
glances at Harold*) Will you put the coat upstairs for me, Mother?

FLORENCE. Let me, Dad. It's all right, Mother.

RAFE. Thanks. Put it at the back—I'll not be needing it for some
time.

FLORENCE (*to Arthur*) I thought you said you'd be working overtime.

ARTHUR. I am. I've got to go back.

FLORENCE. Nothing wrong, is there?

ARTHUR. No. I've just come round to ask you something.

FLORENCE. I expect it'll keep a minute or two. Oh, Dad, I'll
put that cover on it to protect it. (*To Arthur, as she passes*) My dad's
new overcoat. Just look at it. I wish you had one like it.

(FLORENCE *exits* C)

ARTHUR. That looks a gradely bit of topcoating, Mr Crompton.

RAFE (*reading a letter at the desk*) Always buy the best—if you can
afford it—you won't go far wrong. I detest anything cheap or shoddy.

HAROLD. I'll bet it didn't cost much under fifteen quid, Dad!

RAFE. It cost thirty-two guineas.

(DAISY *gives Harold a look and exits to the kitchen with the box*)

HAROLD. Thirty-two guineas! Cash down! Why, for that I could
have bought you a . . .

RAFE (*cutting in*) You couldn't have bought me a better coat. My
suit upstairs cost me twenty-one guineas. I've had it twelve year and
it's like new!

HAROLD. If you have it another nine it'll work out at a guinea a year.

(DAISY *enters from the kitchen and moves* C)

RAFE. So it will. Remember that Welsh flannel shirt I had, Mother—must have worn it about five years regular, and it's still good. (*He puts the letter and bill in the desk and takes out his union book*)

DAISY. It used to be a heck of a job washing it. Is everything all right with you, Arthur?

ARTHUR. I'll tell you better when I've had a word with your Florence.

DAISY. You mustn't mind if she's a bit short with you, Arthur. It's just her way.

ARTHUR. Oh, I know that. I've grown used to it by this.

DAISY. She's a real good lass at heart.

ARTHUR. Aye, I know that too. Or else I wouldn't be here.

DAISY. Have you had something to eat?

ARTHUR. Yes, thank you, Mother. I've had my tea—gammon rashers.

(*The others react.* RAFE *makes notes from his union book*)

DAISY. Well, I expect you could do with another cup of tea.

ARTHUR. Now, don't go to any bother.

DAISY. It's no bother, Arthur.

ARTHUR. Thanks, I do feel a bit dry.

HAROLD. Aye, they're inclined to be salty.

(DAISY *exits to the kitchen, switching on the light*)

HILDA (*rising and offering the chair down* R) Come and sit down here, Arthur, and make yourself at home. You can't be in such a hurry.

ARTHUR. Thanks, Hilda. (*He moves* R, *puts his cap in his pocket, and sits*)

HILDA. You look a bit tired.

ARTHUR. So do you. I mean not as chirpy as usual.

(HILDA *returns to her seat.* HAROLD *and* WILFRED *gaze at Arthur. There is an uncomfortable pause*)

WILFRED. How are things in general, Arthur?

ARTHUR. Oh—er—fair to middlin'.

(WILFRED *and* HAROLD *nod, smiling*)

WILFRED. I see they keep you at it.

ARTHUR. Yes, yes, we keep on the go.

(*Everyone nods enthusiastically*)

HAROLD. Old Aspinall always has plenty of jobs lined up outside.

ARTHUR. Yes, it's our busy time, just before the Easter holiday. But we're nearly straight. (*He takes out a cigarette packet*)

(*The others watch in stunned silence as* ARTHUR *taps the cigarette, puts it in his mouth and feels in his pocket for his lighter.* RAFE *turns.* ARTHUR *quickly replaces the cigarette.* FLORENCE *enters* C)

FLORENCE. Well now, what brought you round?

(ARTHUR *rises and gives* FLORENCE *his seat*)

ARTHUR. I've got some news about old Aspinall.

RAFE. Don't say he's retiring at last!

ARTHUR (*moving* C) How did you guess? He's bought a bungalow at Lytham-St-Annes.

RAFE. He could have bought Lytham-St-Annes itself, the money he's been making out of that tinkering business.

WILFRED. You mean sheet-metal works, Dad.

RAFE. He started out as a tinker, and in my eyes a tinker he'll always be.

ARTHUR. You can set out as one thing—but end up as another.

RAFE. I suppose so—except he's got a tinker mentality. It was in his family.

ARTHUR. I don't care what he has, Mr Crompton—but I will guarantee any job I put my hand to. Any job at all.

HAROLD. There's not many British workmen can say that nowadays, eh, Dad?

RAFE (*locking the desk*) No—not whose word I'd take.

FLORENCE. Is he talking of selling up or something?

ARTHUR (*sitting in the chair down* L *of the table*) Oh, no, he wouldn't sell out. He'll always want a finger in the pie.

(DAISY *enters from the kitchen with a cup of tea and a piece of cake which she hands to Arthur*)

DAISY. Here y'are, Arthur love. Are you sure you wouldn't like something cooked?

HAROLD. Happen a nice fried herring.

(*There is a disapproving reaction from the others*)

ARTHUR. This'll be fine, thanks. I'm not all that partial to fish.

(DAISY *crosses to the kitchen, switches off the light, takes her workbasket from the table* L *and sits in the armchair to darn a sock*)

FLORENCE. If he's not selling up—what is he thinking of doing?

DAISY. Give Arthur time to tell you.

FLORENCE. It's taking him long enough.

ARTHUR. They're going to move to Lytham.

FLORENCE. Where do you come into it?

ARTHUR. Well, in a way, that was what I came to see you about. (*He looks uneasy and rises, putting his cup and plate on the table*) Shall we . . . can we have a word in private?

RAFE. Speak up, Arthur. We don't hide anything in this house.

FLORENCE. Yes, out with it!

ARTHUR. Well, he came round to my bench this afternoon, and he said to me, "I'm on the lookout for somebody as could fill the job of a proper working manager, Arthur, and I need him at once. I've got to have a chap that can estimate jobs and handle the men," he said. "But he must be a man as isn't in a hurry to get home of a night. In short, a married man."

FLORENCE. Oh—I see.

RAFE. What has he got behind his mind?

ARTHUR. Then he said he'd be willing to put me in charge, if me and your Florence would get wed—soon like. Tie the whole thing up, you see.

RAFE. Aye, but suppose she doesn't want to get married in a rush.

DAISY. It's not as though they're strangers—they've been engaged a year.

RAFE. What's a year in a lifetime?

WILFRED. You grab him, Flo, while you've got the chance.

RAFE. When we need your advice we'll ask you. Who does Alf Aspinall think he is—dictating to folk just when they should get married?

FLORENCE. Yes, just because he's found the right bungalow at Lytham. We've not enough money saved up, have we? Not for such a rush.

DAISY. There's time when you've got to take a chance.

RAFE. There's enough chances to marriage without taking any extra ones.

HAROLD. It's an offer not to be sneezed at.

RAFE. Nobody's sneezing. And I'll thank you not to dip your nib where there's no ink.

DAISY (rising and fetching Rafe's old overcoat, cap and scarf from the hall) I must say it doesn't seem at all unreasonable to me, Arthur.

ARTHUR. No, it's just that he'd be more content with a married man in charge.

RAFE. 'Course he would. You've got a better hold on a man once he's married. A wife, children—all hostages to fortune.

(DAISY helps RAFE on with his overcoat)

ARTHUR. No, I don't think he wants a hold on me. He'd just like to get it settled.

RAFE. Look, Arthur, I don't mind what he asks you, or tells you to do. (He attempts to put his L hand in his sleeve, but stops to gesture) But what does he imagine I am—that I'd let one of my daughters marry at the bidding of a tinker.

ARTHUR. I don't know what he imagines you are, Mr Crompton.

RAFE. You take things lying down in this life, and every upstart will trample over you. (He gets his coat on)

(DAISY moves L to the desk)

FLORENCE. What do you think? What extra would you get out of it?

ARTHUR (*sitting again*) I think it'd be a fifty-bob a week rise. A staff job, see—paid work or play.

RAFE. Aye, but not for overtime.

DAISY. You can't have everything.

ARTHUR. There'd be no broken weeks for illness or nowt like that. And I might get him to meet me half-way on overtime.

RAFE. You wouldn't want our Florence to go on teaching once she were married.

ARTHUR. If I know your Florence she'll do as she thinks fit. Not what I want.

WILFRED. It's up to you to put your foot down.

HAROLD. Why shouldn't she teach? The government is going mad for married teachers.

RAFE. I'd certainly never let a wife of mine go out to work.

HAROLD (*aside*) She wouldn't have time.

(RAFE *slowly turns to Harold.* DAISY *intercepts him, handing him his scarf*)

RAFE. If I couldn't keep a wife I wouldn't get wed.

DAISY. Things have changed, Dad. There's no shame to it in these times. (*She hands Rafe his cap, then returns to her seat c and darns*)

WILFRED (*moving down* L) 'Course, if they had youngsters soon she couldn't.

RAFE. What's that?

HAROLD. He said if they had youngsters soon she couldn't.

FLORENCE (*rising*) Give us time to get married.

WILFRED. Oh, I meant inside matrimony.

HAROLD (*hitting Wilfred with his paper*) Shut up, Wilf.

(FLORENCE *rises and stands behind her chair*)

DAISY. Two-pounds-ten a week is a very good rise.

RAFE. Aye, but no overtime pay.

ARTHUR. It's not just the rise, you know. There'd be that gable-end house to go with it.

FLORENCE. It's not quite what I had in mind.

DAISY. But it's a marvellous start in these days, love. What some folk wouldn't give for that!

ARTHUR. He had a new bath put in about a year ago, and beautified throughout. A give-away rent, and no travelling.

HAROLD. Aye, houses aren't easy to come by.

ARTHUR. And a free telephone.

RAFE. That house simply means that you and our Florence would act as unpaid watchmen for Mr Alf Aspinall's premises. He's got you there, living on the job. Folk knocking day and night. And keep answering the free telephone.

ARTHUR. I like my job. I'm not a clock watcher. I don't mind doing a bit extra. And it struck me we might buy ourselves a caravan near the coast—and we could get away at week-ends. You can't have it all ways. (*He looks from Florence to Rafe, but gets nothing*)

RAFE. That's your side of the matter, Arthur. And there's a lot to be said for it, I admit. But what I wouldn't stand for is the way he's going about it. Does he think I've brought my daughter up all these years, then he'll decide just when she'll get married? He must think we're living in feudal times.

ARTHUR. I don't know what he thinks, Mr Crompton. I'm all mithered.

RAFE. Aye, I would be, in your shoes. I know what I'd say to any boss who tried to tell me when I should get married! He wouldn't tell me twice!

ARTHUR. He didn't actually tell me.

RAFE. That's even worse—he's trying to wheedle you into it.

ARTHUR. It all sounds different now—the way you put it, Mr Crompton.

DAISY (*rising and moving to the door up* c) Now, don't get yourself late for your union, Dad.

RAFE. Eh? Oh—don't worry about that, Mother. If there's not a full quorum I'll break up the meeting. (*He puts his union book in his pocket and moves to the door*)

WILFRED. Not again, Dad!

RAFE. I believe in sticking by the rules. They were put there for a purpose. An' yon new secretary is getting a bit high-handed. They're all the same once they get in office. (*Moving down stage*) Same as I say, about marriage—there's nothing to just getting wed. They'll do you at any registry office for twelve-and-six.

HAROLD. Seventeen-and-six, it's gone up.

RAFE. Seventeen-and-six then—but to make a decent home in life—one in which a family can grow—that needs careful preparation. If you're the lass I think you are, Florence, you'll tell Mr Alf Aspinall when a Crompton gets married they choose the time—not him!

HAROLD. I can't see what you have to worry about!

RAFE. Eh? That's my business. Let's say I don't want a slight from a tinker. No offence to you, Arthur. You're only doing the errand you've been sent on. Good night, Mother. Good night, everybody.

FLORENCE. Good night, Dad.

WILFRED. Ta ra, Dad.

(DAISY *and* RAFE *exit* c)

DAISY (*off*) Go careful now, Dad.

(RAFE *is heard going through the front door*, DAISY *seeing him to the gate*)

HILDA. Good night and good shuttance!

(HAROLD *rises and hands out cigarettes to Arthur and Wilfred*)

HAROLD. What a pity families have fathers! Cigarette, Arthur?
Homes would be so much happier without 'em.
HILDA. This one would—that's for sure.
FLORENCE. You'd notice it if he were gone.

(ARTHUR *and* WILFRED *light their cigarettes*)

HAROLD. Aye, I noticed when that boil went from the back of
my neck—but I'm a damn sight happier without it.
ARTHUR. I don't think you handle him right. You should tell
him straight to his face.
WILFRED. See what happened to you when you did that!
ARTHUR. I feel I put my case very badly.
HAROLD. He took it very badly.
HILDA (*rising to above the table*) Our Florence, I think you must be
out of your mind turning Arthur down like that.
WILFRED. So do I!
FLORENCE. Who says I'm turning him down? Don't jump to
conclusions.
HILDA. You didn't sound all that keen.
FLORENCE (*plumping the cushions on the sofa*) I've got to think it
over, haven't I? I don't believe in rushing things.
ARTHUR. Well, I admit it's sudden—in one way.
HILDA (*moving to L of Arthur*) You wouldn't have to ask me twice,
Arthur.
WILFRED. Me neither.
HAROLD (*looking Wilfred up and down*) Wilfred!
WILFRED. I mean if I were a woman.
HAROLD (*smiling*) The bride was given away by that well-known
plastic surgeon . . .
WILFRED. Oh, shut up! I only meant . . .

(DAISY *enters* C. HAROLD *sits on the edge of the table*. WILFRED
stands at the piano)

HILDA. Mum, what have you done with that bloody herring?
FLORENCE. Hilda!

(FLORENCE *and* ARTHUR *sit on the sofa and talk together,* FLORENCE
up stage)

DAISY. What for, love?
HAROLD. She's come over peckish.
HILDA. Peckish? I'll fling the rotten thing behind the fire!
HAROLD. You wouldn't dare.
HILDA. Who wouldn't? I'll show you.
WILFRED. Now then, love, you'll only get my mum into trouble.
DAISY. Ee, I don't mind, love. I'm used to it. I'll go and make
you a nice egg and bacon sandwich.

HILDA. I don't think I could eat one.

DAISY. You'll feel better when you've had something to eat. Excuse me, Arthur.

(DAISY *exits to the kitchen*)

HAROLD. Now suppose there's not a full quorum and he comes back an' catches you scoffing double deckers?

HILDA. I tell you I don't care a tinker's cuss for him. Pardon the expression, Arthur. (*She sits on the* L *arm of the* R *armchair*)

ARTHUR (*half rising*) Don't mind me!

WILFRED. Arthur's a welder—not a tinker.

HAROLD. She doesn't care a welder's cuss!

HILDA. And I'm the only one in the family who doesn't care for him.

HAROLD (*sitting on the* R *arm of Rafe's armchair*) I'm not worrying about you. It's old Daisy—she's the one who has to carry the can back when owt goes wrong. She's going humpbacked as it is with worry.

WILFRED. Aye, poor old Mum is the one who catches out in the end.

HILDA. Oh, blast him! Sorry, Arthur, for going off—you must think we're a right funny lot.

ARTHUR. Not particularly. (*He puts his cigarette out on his shoe*)

WILFRED. Thanks, Arthur.

FLORENCE. It's just our Hilda—I think she must be having a bout of growing pains.

HILDA. Oh, am I—then it's high time you had a bout of 'em too! Perhaps you wouldn't be as bloomin' stuffy as you are.

(ARTHUR *reacts*)

HAROLD. Don't worry, Arthur. I think she's got a touch of the spring.

FLORENCE And she's been on port wine.

HAROLD. Oh, aye—spring an' port wine—enough to go to any girl's head. (*He flicks Hilda's hair*)

HILDA (*rising and facing Arthur*) I'll tell you what it is, Arthur, it's our rotten old father . . .

WILFRED. Hilda, love . . .

FLORENCE (*rising*) Hilda—what a thing to come out with!

HILDA (*moving up stage*) I'm not ashamed to tell it—it's Mr Big-head Crompton who insists I've got to eat a bloomin' cold stinking herring that's out there on the kitchen shelf.

FLORENCE (*moving to the head of the table*) Our Hilda—don't talk like that!

HILDA. Oh, dry up. If you heard the girls in the mill going on you'd realize how behind the times we are. Why, Betty Partington is off to an all-night rave up tonight!

FLORENCE. When I hear you talk of the times I'm glad I'm behind them.

WILFRED. Aye, but don't hold others back.

HAROLD (*rising*) All-night twist party! What about it, Arthur? Fancy your chances? There'll be plenty of young stuff there.

ARTHUR (*half rising*) Aye, I wouldn't mind . . .

FLORENCE. You'll stay where you are. (*To Hilda*) Is that what you want—all-night parties?

HILDA. She won't get home till tomorrow dinner-time—yet nothing will be said. I'd like to see his face if I suggested it.

FLORENCE. Yes, because your father cares for you.

HILDA. He cares for his bloomin' self . . .

WILFRED. No—I think he honestly cares.

HILDA. Then he's a funny way of showing it.

FLORENCE (*sitting on the sofa*) I'm sorry about her, Arthur. How's your mother keeping?

ARTHUR. It's all right. I understand how your Hilda feels. My mother's all right except when her back's plaguing her.

HAROLD (*to Florence*) Now you know.

HILDA (*to Florence*) It's your own father you should feel ashamed of—not me. What do you say, Harold? (*She sits on the L arm of the C chair*)

HAROLD (*moving to the table and sitting astride the chair L of it*) Arthur, do you know in this day and age we're expected to hand over to him the best part of our wages every Friday? To him!

FLORENCE (*rising*) Do you lot want keeping for nothing? It's same as my dad says—it's not a lodging house—it's a home—and a good one too.

WILFRED. Even a bad home is better than none at all.

FLORENCE. You try and find digs as good as your own home—you'll see what they'll charge you in these days!

(WILFRED *wanders down stage*)

HAROLD. I've a good mind to! I have—honest.

ARTHUR. I think I would if I were you, Harold. I'd go out and get myself a room somewhere.

HAROLD. Aye, I would, only I don't fancy living on my own in a furnished room—listening to my own jokes like.

WILFRED. I can't say I blame you. (*He flicks ash into the fire, then wanders* L)

ARTHUR. If you don't think handing over is right, Harold, you tell him. I would.

FLORENCE (*to Arthur*) Don't be so liberal with our advice. You're not a member of the family yet! (*She moves above the table*)

HILDA (*to Arthur*) God help you on that day! (*To Harold*) Yes—you great soft ha'porth—if you'd had enough guts you'd have stood up to him before this.

WILFRED. 'Course he would!

FLORENCE. Why—what has our Harold to stand up for? Eh? Greyhounds tonight—Wanderers tomorrow afternoon—boozing tomorrow night and Sunday the strip club.

HAROLD (*unabashed*) Every man to his taste. I'm doing nobody any harm.

FLORENCE. Have you never thought of doing some good, for a change?

HAROLD. Not when I look at him and see where it gets you. Besides, think of the fun I get going my way and spiting him.

ARTHUR. A man's only as big as you let him be. I'd stand up to him.

FLORENCE. Would you? I very much doubt it.

HAROLD. So do I—come to that.

HILDA (*rising; to Florence*) You think there's no-one like him!

HAROLD. There isn't, thank God. Oh, but come Sunday teatime and he gets one of his old-time moods on him, I'll bet you'll be standing there by the piano singing Handel with him!

WILFRED. Aye, I wouldn't be surprised. He can be very persuasive.

HILDA. Me! If ever I sing with that one again I hope the first note chokes me. (*She moves up to the piano*)

ARTHUR. Hilda, love . . . !

WILFRED. Don't talk like that, love. It's not like you.

FLORENCE (*to Arthur*) I don't know what's come over our Hilda lately.

HAROLD. It's all come about since her Donald threw her over.

HILDA. I threw him over—if you want to know.

HAROLD (*singing to the tune of "Allan Water"*)
          For his bride
          A soldier sought her,
WILFRED. You mean a flight sergeant.
HAROLD.   But a sergeant false was he,
          On the banks of Allan Water,
          None so fair as she.
          On the banks . . .

(WILFRED *gestures to Harold to be quiet*)

HILDA (*shouting*) Stop it! (*She runs to Harold and shakes his shoulder*) Stop it! Leave me alone. (*She runs L, sits on the pouffe and sobs*)

(DAISY *enters from the kitchen and goes to pick up the cup and plate*)

DAISY. Hilda, love, your tea's nearly ready. Ee, what's come over you, child?

ARTHUR (*crossing to Hilda and putting his hands on her shoulders*) Now then, Hilda, love, don't let yourself get upset like that.

HILDA (*sobbing*) Sorry, Arthur. (*She puts her hand on his*)

ARTHUR. Have your cry out, love, and then go and have your tea. You'll feel fine then.

HILDA. I wish you'd come and ask me to marry you, Arthur. I'd be packed and out of that door with you by this.

WILFRED. But he hasn't. So have your tea instead.

HAROLD. I'm sorry I upset you about Donald, love. It might not be too late—if she turns him down you can move in . . . Blimey! (*Rising*) I've nearly missed the first race. See you, Arthur.

(HAROLD *takes his cap from the piano and exits to the kitchen*)

DAISY. Wilf, it's nearly seven.

WILFRED. What? Oh, Betsy Jane! I'd better go and stake my claim.

(WILFRED *exits to the kitchen and puts his cigarette out*)

DAISY. Better not leave it too late, Hilda, we mustn't let your bacon burn.

HILDA (*rising*) No, we mustn't.

(HAROLD *enters the scullery and rubs up his shoes*)

ARTHUR (*moving up stage, taking his cap from his pocket*) Ee, I'd better be off, too. I'll have to make a dash for it.

DAISY. Didn't you come to ask our Florence something?

ARTHUR. Did I? Yes, I suppose I did.

DAISY (*taking Arthur's cap and putting it on the piano stool*) Then don't go without your answer. Come on, Hilda, we don't want to be in the way.

(DAISY *and* HILDA *exit to the kitchen.* WILFRED *enters the scullery*)

HAROLD (*putting on his scarf and cap*) I'll lay you two to one she turns him down.

(FLORENCE *fetches her briefcase, sits at the head of the table, puts on her spectacles, and starts to mark exercise books*)

WILFRED. Who?

HAROLD. Our Florence, you nit, turns Arthur down. And I'll give you even money our Hilda nips in and takes her place.

WILFRED. If Florence doesn't marry Arthur she'll marry nobody.

HAROLD. Your sister Flo is father-fixated. If I know anything, she'll be living here, looking after her dad, when he's bloody ninety.

WILFRED. Aye, and if I know anything, the way you're going on, you'll be keeping 'em company!

(WILFRED *and* HAROLD *exit through the back door*)

ARTHUR. Well, Florence, what shall I tell old Aspinall?

FLORENCE. I'm not sure. It's same as Dad says—you don't want to go rushing blindly into marriage.

ARTHUR. We're not all that blind, are we? I say, don't you think he's taking things a bit far with your Hilda . . .

FLORENCE. Don't mention that herring again to me!

ARTHUR. Stomachs are very funny things.

FLORENCE. Only when they get out of hand.

ARTHUR. Have you noticed anything different about your Hilda lately?

FLORENCE! Such as what?

ARTHUR. I don't know. It was just a feeling I got. She seems older in some way, different like.

FLORENCE. I'll tell you what I did notice. I noticed how you took her in your arms.

ARTHUR. You mean when she was crying? You didn't mind that, did you?

FLORENCE. No—I didn't mind—except the thought struck me at that moment—you never take me in your arms like that—do you?

ARTHUR. Well, you never cry. I've to see the first time yet.

FLORENCE. That doesn't mean to say there aren't times when I could cry.

ARTHUR. I know you hold yourself in a lot. It's not always for the best.

FLORENCE. I can only be as I am. You're very fond of our Hilda, aren't you?

ARTHUR. Yes, I suppose I am. Why?

FLORENCE. Perhaps you're more fond of her than you are of me?

ARTHUR. Aye, it could be, could be.

FLORENCE. Happen you've got engaged to the wrong one?

ARTHUR. Aye, I might have. You never know.

FLORENCE. Oh! I see. Thanks for being honest.

ARTHUR. Not at all. But there is one little difference. When I go off to work now, I shan't be thinking of your Hilda, I'll be thinking of you. When I close my eyes at night, I don't see your Hilda, I see you. I am very fond of your Hilda, but I love you, and I can't live without you.

FLORENCE. Oh, Arthur! (*She takes off her glasses and looks at him*)

ARTHUR. And I don't care a damn about the job—the house—old Aspinall—or, come to that, your domineering, know-all father!

(FLORENCE *is unexpectedly touched, and rises.* ARTHUR *and* FLORENCE *approach each other and embrace passionately.* HILDA *enters from the kitchen just taking a big bite at a sandwich. She stops dead, her mouth full, and stares at the pair, unseen by them, then starts to back stealthily into the kitchen. The door up* C *opens and* RAFE *enters*)

RAFE. Mother—I'm back. There wasn't a full . . . (*He spots the couple and stops*)

(FLORENCE *tries to break away from the embrace and looks from Arthur to Rafe.* DAISY *enters from the kitchen*)

DAISY. Ee—Dad—so you broke up the . . .

DAISY *breaks off when she sees Rafe staring at Arthur and Florence Then it strikes her that she had better push Hilda out of sight, which she does, as* RAFE *looks across and—*

the CURTAIN *falls*

ACT II

Scene i

SCENE—*The same. Sunday, teatime.*

The home has a Sunday look. There are spring flowers in vases and the table is laid for high tea, with the best cloth and the best china. The piano stool is now placed down L of the table.

When the CURTAIN *rises, church bells are ringing.* WILFRED, *wearing a white shirt, tie and pullover, is seated on the television chair down L, reading the "News of the World".* DAISY *enters from the kitchen wearing a nice frock and Dutch apron, and carrying a large cake which she puts on the table.*

WILFRED. Hy, Mum!

DAISY. Yes, love?

WILFRED. Did Betsy Jane come in like she said?

DAISY. You mean with the five pounds?

WILFRED. Yes.

DAISY. I'm afraid not, but she promised me she'd let us have it back for certain tomorrow morning.

WILFRED. I can't wait till then. It means I won't see it till tomorrow night. I'm all but skint.

(DAISY *goes to her handbag on the sideboard and gets out three pound notes*)

DAISY (*crossing to Wilfred*) Here you are, love, your three pounds.

WILFRED. What? Oh, no, Mum, I can't take it! It'll only get you in a mess.

DAISY. Go on—I let you in for it.

WILFRED (*taking the notes*) Ta. Very good of you. I don't know how you do it.

DAISY. Neither do I.

WILFRED. How will she get it?

DAISY. I don't care how she gets it so long as she hands me my five pounds back. I've had a very dodgy week-end, one way and another.

WILFRED. Aye—and it's not over yet! I say, Mum, surely my dad won't have our Hilda's herring stuck in front of her at Sunday tea table?

DAISY. You know your dad—once he sets his mind on something, it takes a bit of shifting.

WILFRED. You kidding! When I saw you fetch that thing out at dinner-time I coulda dropped with the shock. There we all were with our plates of roast beef and Yorkshire!

DAISY (*sitting in the armchair* C) She'll not starve while I'm around.

WILFRED. You've gotta hand it to him—when he says something he means it. But what is it makes him go like that, Mum, blind to everything except what he has his mind on?

DAISY. He's always been the same—he's got to work things out of his system.

WILFRED. Then he should take a dose of Epsom salts. Besides, it's getting a bit high.

DAISY. I agree it's not a nice thing to put in front of somebody.

WILFRED (*rising*) It's a bloody shame. That's what it is. Is there nothing you can do?

DAISY. It'll have to sort itself out.

WILFRED. It'll never sort itself out. Summat's got to be done.

DAISY. Don't let your dad catch you with the *News of the World*.

(HILDA *enters up* C)

WILFRED (*moving up* L) I don't care what the hell he catches me with. I've stood about enough of that fellow. Hello, Hilda.

HILDA. Hello, Wilf.

(WILFRED *exits to the kitchen*)

What's up with our Wilf, Mum?

DAISY. Have a nice rest, love?

HILDA (*sitting on the arm of Rafe's chair*) I had a good read and a good think.

DAISY. He's worried about you.

HILDA. I wish he wouldn't take on so for me.

(WILFRED *enters the scullery and goes out through the back door*)

DAISY. He always has done. (*Rising and moving up* L) Hold on a tick. I've got you something nice.

(DAISY *exits to the kitchen*)

HILDA (*calling*) I noticed it at dinner-time. He hardly touched his meat. (*Her eyes fall on a book of poetry on Rafe's chair. She picks it up and opens it*)

(DAISY *enters with a plate covered with a napkin*)

DAISY. Beef sandwiches. I did 'em on the sly. Get 'em down you afore he gets back.

HILDA (*rising and moving up stage*) Where's he gone?

DAISY. Taking his Sunday constitutional round the moors. Remember the time when he used to insist on taking us all with him —oh, my poor legs. (*She pushes the plate at Hilda*)

HILDA (*putting the poetry book on the piano*) No, thanks, Mum—I won't have anything to eat.

DAISY. You won't? Why not? Aren't you hungry?

HILDA. I've made a resolution.

DAISY. What about?

HILDA. I'm resolved to eat that flamin' herring, Mum!

DAISY (*moving to the pouffe and sitting*) Ee, you're not, are you? You mean you're going to give way?

HILDA. I feel I can't stand it much longer. All the tension like. It's not just for myself—I'd starve to death sooner than give in— it's what it does to the home.

DAISY. Aye, there's something about your dad as can drive you that way—round the bend, as they say. Yet he means well, bless him.

HILDA. Have you felt it, Mum?

DAISY. Felt it! Ee, child, there's been times when I've felt so pulled out of myself, among the lot of you, that I've wished I could go and live amongst strangers for a week or two, just to get my bearings again. But a mother has to keep these feelings to herself.

HILDA. Whenever there's trouble you've always had to act as *buffer between him and us.*

DAISY. That's what I'm here for.

HILDA. Life's not been easy for you, Mum, with him.

DAISY. I've had my happy times, love. And I've brought a lot of the rest of it on myself. Here, shall I tell you something—you'll no sooner put your fork into that herring than he'll up and say: "It's all right, Hilda. Don't eat it! Don't touch it!" I know him. He can't stand being bested. Then he's sorry once he's bested you.

(HAROLD *passes the window to the front door*)

HILDA. Ah, but that's where I catch him! I don't care what he says—once I start I'll not give way. I'll devour every tiny morsel of that bloomin' herring—yes—skin, tail, fins—the lot—even if it makes me sick! I'll put him through it.

DAISY. Peace in the home at last.

(HAROLD *enters* C. DAISY *and* HILDA *are startled and try to hide the sandwiches. The light starts to fade slowly as dusk falls*)

HAROLD. Aye-aye! Now what're you two scheming up?

DAISY. You gave me a shock.

HILDA. Yes, I thought it was him.

HAROLD. Who—old droopy-drawers? He'll be in shortly. I saw him stepping it out, and I spotted Arthur and our Florence hanging well behind, keeping out of his reach.

HILDA. I can't say I blame them.

DAISY. Poor dad, always on his own.

HAROLD. You get as you prefer his room to his company. Mum, did you *have* to marry him?

DAISY. How dare you!

HILDA. Our Harold!

HAROLD: No, I didn't mean it like that. I mean could you not find yourself somebody better?

DAISY. He was a handsome young man in those days, was your dad. He'd make two of you.

HAROLD. Gaa—him!

HILDA. Talking about marriage—have our Florence and Arthur decided on it?

DAISY. Not as I know of for sure. But I thought our Florence was looking different . . .

HAROLD. The same thought struck me—sort of hopeful like. She was clutching on to Arthur's arm.

HILDA. She's got to make up her mind between him and my dad. (*Moving to the kitchen*) I'll get these out of the way.

HAROLD. Oh, it's like that, is it? Just fancy!

(HILDA *exits to the kitchen with the sandwiches*)

Hy, Mum, has old Guinness-guts handed over yet?

DAISY. Betsy Jane? No, but she will for certain in the morning.

HAROLD. I'll have a job to wait. I've run out of fags as it is.

(DAISY *rises and goes to her handbag*)

DAISY. Here you are, love, your two pounds.

HAROLD. No, Mum, I can't take it.

DAISY. Here you are—it was on my behalf.

HAROLD. Ta. Now, are you sure you can spare it?

DAISY. No—I can't. But I'll have to.

HAROLD. I'm not codding—you can have it back.

DAISY. I'll just about manage till tomorrow morning. But I'm beginning to see there's a lot in what your dad says—"neither a borrower nor a lender be".

HAROLD. Aye, except the loss of the friend in Betsy Jane's case would be a positive advantage.

(RAFE *approaches the front door*)

Blimey, here he is—I'll be off.

(HAROLD *exits to the kitchen.* RAFE *enters the front door.* DAISY *opens the door up* C. RAFE *hangs his cap up on the hallstand. He is wearing a tweedy suit and cap, and carries a sprig of white heather*)

DAISY. Hello, Dad. You're back in time for tea.

RAFE (*entering the room*) Good. I'm ready for it. (*Looking round*) Is our Hilda in?

DAISY. Yes. She's in the kitchen.

RAFE. Look what I found you on the moors—a sprig of white heather.

DAISY. Oh, how nice! Let's hope it brings me luck. (*She kisses Rafe*)

Rafe. I've had time to think things over and I fancy the lesson has gone home.

Daisy (*closing the door and putting the heather in her buttonhole*) What lesson? Oh, you mean with our Hilda and the herring?

Rafe (*sitting in his armchair*) Aye.

(Daisy *moves down* c)

It was a bit of a challenge, see, and I wasn't going to back down. But it's served its purpose. And d'you know, I couldn't say I've enjoyed a meal since it started. At our age we can't stand up to tension same as the young 'uns.

Daisy. So you don't want me to bother with the herring any more?

Rafe. Eh? But of course you must bring the herring in. She mustn't get the idea in her head she's bested me.

Daisy. What then? What do you want? I'm getting at my wits' end.

Rafe. If you are, don't let them see it—they don't think we're supposed to have any human weaknesses. You fetch the herring in, see, and put it in front of her. Now if she so much as touches her knife and fork, I'll whip that herring away. To be honest with you I'm fed up with the sight of the damn thing myself.

Daisy. No more than I am!

Rafe. You know, I never really intended her to have to eat it.

Daisy. Well, she wasn't to know that.

Rafe. It was the way she pushed it aside got me.

Daisy. She'd had some port wine.

Rafe. I could see the rot setting in—because once she got away with it the others 'ud start, an' the next thing our mealtimes would be like feeding the monkeys at the zoo. I've seen homes like that. I know that in these days it's the fashion to give way to your children, but nobody's convinced me on that score yet.

Daisy. It must have seemed harsh to the poor girl.

Rafe. I agree—but I knew she'd her mother to fall back on and wouldn't go hungry. I may see her need, but I'd never see her bleed. I hope I'm not that heartless.

Daisy (*sitting on the* l *arm of the armchair* c) Yes, but you know our Hilda's not one for giving way. She's as stubborn . . .

Rafe. I know. She's as stubborn as her father.

(Rafe *and* Daisy *clasp hands*)

They say the apple doesn't fall far from the tree, and I love her all the more for it, though I don't let her see it. But I had no choice over making a stand. If your children once beat you—you're licked for good. The young have no respect for weakness. And they're growing stronger as you're getting older. They soon take your measure. Why, even a six-months-old child knows when it's the boss.

(Florence *and* Arthur *are seen entering the front door*)

Daisy. It shouldn't be a battle, Dad—bringing up a family.
Rafe. I realize that now. Happen I started off on the wrong foot.
'Course, when I look round at other families I begin to ask myself
if there's a right foot. They seem no better than we are.
Daisy. Times have changed, Dad.
Rafe. Don't I know! When I was a lad the old and the young
shared a world in common. But the young of today seem to think
they have nothing at all in common with us. Well, I wonder.

(Florence *enters up* c. Arthur *follows, closing the door. They are
both wearing suits*)

Daisy (*rising*) Are you back, love? Hello, Arthur.
Florence (*moving up* r) Hello, Mother. You beat us, Dad.
Rafe. Yes, Florence, I did.
Daisy (*moving up* l) I'd better get the tea.

(Daisy *exits to the kitchen*)

(Florence (*taking off her jacket and putting it over the chair up* l *of the
table*) Had a good walk, Dad?
Rafe. I've done a few miles. I've been right across the moors and
down by the Scotsman's Stump.
Arthur. It's lovely round there.

(Harold *enters up* c. *He and* Arthur *nod to each other*)

Rafe. The air's like wine. What folk want to go abroad for I
don't know. They seem to have no love or pride in their own country-
side these days. Tramping those moors you get all sorts of ideas
going through your head. (*Rising*) That reminds me, I've had
Handel's "Largo" in my mind all afternoon.

(Daisy *enters from the kitchen with the trolley.* Harold *goes to help
her wheel it in.* Rafe *takes the piano-stool from the table to the piano,
takes some music from inside it, and sits at the piano*)

Harold. Hello, Arthur.
Arthur. Hello, Harold.
Harold. How's tricks?
Arthur. Very well, thank you.
Harold. Good, good. Here, left hand down a bit, Mother.

(Harold *and* Daisy *lay out the salad plates on the table. Six plates
have meat on them. The seventh, Hilda's, is empty.* Florence *switches
on the centre and desk lights.* Rafe *plays the introduction, then stops*)

Rafe. Mother, it's been some time since we heard you sing.
Daisy. Ee, I'm rusty. I was just going to brew the tea.
Rafe. Tea can wait. Come on, Mother. (*He is quite infectious at
these times*) Let's have a bit of the old days . . . (*He clears his throat*)

(Daisy *has no choice. She wipes her hands on her apron.* Florence *is*

eager to join in and pulls ARTHUR *in.* DAISY *beckons* HAROLD, *and he
also joins in with a sigh. They all gather round the piano.* RAFE *has a
good voice, and the singing is moving*)

ALL (*singing*)   Slumber, dear maid!

(*During the song,* HILDA *enters from the kitchen, takes a paperback
book from the desk, moves* R, *switches on the standard lamp and sits on the
sofa, refusing to sing. A moment or two later* WILFRED *enters by the back
door, then comes quietly in from the kitchen and sees the others gathered
round the piano. He goes quietly to the fireplace, picks up the cat from the
basket in which it has been sleeping unnoticed (or he brings the "real" cat
on with him), and creeps back to the kitchen. At the door, he turns to be
sure that no one has seen him. A moment later he appears in the scullery
carrying the cat and the herring. He puts them both outside the back door,
hurries back to the living-room and joins loudly in the singing. He gets one
or two glances from the others*)

> Green boughs will cover thee,
> Calm airs breathe over thee,
> Where thou art laid.
> Slumber, dear maid!
> Green boughs will cover thee,
> Calm airs breathe over thee,
> Where thou art laid
> Slumber then peacefully,
> O gentle maid!
> Green boughs will cover thee,
> Calm airs breathe over thee,
> Where thou art laid.
> Where thou art laid.

WILFRED. Dad, you were in good voice.

(HAROLD *moves to the table and continues laying*)

RAFE (*turning on the stool to face front and studying the music book*) Aye,
you should always do a thing when the impulse is on you.

WILFRED. That's what I always say, Dad.

DAISY. I'll get the tea.

(DAISY *exits to the kitchen*)

WILFRED. I didn't know you could sing, Arthur.

ARTHUR. Neither did I.

RAFE (*rising to sit on the* R *arm of his chair; singing*) King of Kings,
hallelujah, bum, hallelujah, bum, bum, bum.

ARTHUR. It's funny how you don't hear families singing these
days.

HAROLD (*sitting in his place at the table*) Not unless they're drunk.

(FLORENCE *gives the piano stool to* ARTHUR, *who replaces it below
the table* L)

RAFE. It's like everything else—they want it done for 'em.

FLORENCE (*moving to* R *of Rafe*) Dad, remember they used to have lovely concerts at St Saviour's Hall?

RAFE. Aye, there was some good life in the town those days.

HAROLD. They've changed that into a bingo hall now. Chap that's taken it over has made a fortune.

(FLORENCE *goes to her place at the table*)

RAFE. Aye, the whole place is becoming a hive of bingo halls an' bettin' shops. Gambling will be the ruination of this country. It breaks my heart to see what moral decay a bit of prosperity brings with it.

HAROLD. I suppose it's every man to his taste . . .

(ARTHUR *moves down* R)

RAFE. Don't talk daft. What sort of state do you think the world would be in if you left everybody to their taste? Just think of the things they'd get up to.

WILFRED (*moving to* L *of Rafe*) What things Dad?,

RAFE. You needn't ask. Haven't you read your *News of the World* today?

(WILFRED *moves away to the top of the table*)

I know what I'd do in this country if I had my way.

WILFRED (*affably*) What's that, Dad?

RAFE. I'd have every man, woman and child listen to the *Messiah* tonight. Just think of it—in every church and hall all over the country—listening to "He Shall Feed His Flock"!

ARTHUR. Yes, but what good would that do?

RAFE (*rising*) A great spiritual experience. People are starved in their souls. You'd waken up to a new civilization tomorrow. (*He moves to his place above the table*)

WILFRED. 'Course you would. Stands to reason.

ARTHUR (*sitting ln the piano stool*) What about them as didn't like it, Mr Crompton?

(DAISY *enters with the teapot and puts it on the table*. HILDA *rises and goes to her place. All except* RAFE *and* DAISY *sit*)

RAFE. It seems a hard thing to say, but you could dispense with 'em.

DAISY. Well, that seems to be everything.

RAFE (*looking at Hilda's place*) Mother, I believe you've forgotten something.

DAISY (*looking*) Oh, so I have! I'd forget my head if it was loose.

(DAISY *exits to the kitchen*)

RAFE. A chap who remained unmoved after hearing "I Know

My Redeemer Liveth" could hardly be moved if you gave him a
whack with a fourteen-pound hammer.

WILFRED (*laughing loudly*) You're a right comic, Dad.

(*Every one looks at Wilfred.* RAFE *sits above the table.* DAISY *enters
with an empty plate, muttering*)

RAFE. Am I . . . !

DAISY (*to herself*) Ee, I don't know—that beats me! Where could
it have got to? (*She gives Harold a look*)

HAROLD. What're you staring at me for, Mum?

DAISY. I'm not staring at you.

HAROLD. Then I musta been staring at you.

RAFE. What's up, Mother?

DAISY. Our Hilda's herring . . .

RAFE. Oh aye, what about it?

DAISY. I've just been for it and found it gone.

(*There is a reaction at the table*)

RAFE. Gone? Gone where?

DAISY. Gone. It's disappeared. I think the cat must have got it.

RAFE. The cat! Got it off the shelf—how could it?

DAISY. Well, it's not on the plate. (*She has another look to make sure*)

RAFE. Stop! (*Rising*) Stop! I'm going to get to the bottom of this.
Nobody start.

(RAFE *exits to the kitchen, then enters the scullery*)

HAROLD. That cat better have nine lives.

(DAISY *sits at her place at the table*)

ARTHUR. If I know anything it's going to lose one now.

WILFRED. He doesn't want to be too severe on it.

(*Everyone looks at Wilfred.* RAFE *opens the back door, goes outside,
then returns holding the remains of the herring. He takes it through into
the living-room*)

RAFE. Anybody know anything about this?

HAROLD. Looks like the cat's been at it.

WILFRED. No doubt about it—I'd say.

RAFE. Aye, but who gave it to the cat? That's what I'm going to
find out.

DAISY. I don't suppose anybody gave it. It must have took it.

RAFE. No cat of mine ever took things, unless they were given
'em. They all knew better. (*He puts the bones on the plate and replaces
it in the kitchen*)

DAISY. But it must have.

FLORENCE. It always has been a funny cat.

RAFE. Mother, when did you last see this herring?

DAISY. Do you mean before the cat took it?

RAFE. I mean before it disappeared.

DAISY. I saw it just before I made the salad. I left the herring in the kitchen because I thought it wouldn't look too nice on the table. When I was going back in the kitchen you asked me to join in the singing, and I did. That's when it must have grabbed it.

RAFE. We'll come to when it grabbed it later. (*He turns to Florence and Arthur*) Now then, you two were singing?

FLORENCE. But of course, Dad.

ARTHUR. I was doing my best.

RAFE (*to Harold*) How about you?

HAROLD. I was yodelling away.

RAFE (*to Hilda*) How about you? You sat were across there. (*He wipes his hands on his napkin*)

DAISY (*interposing*) It couldn't have been our Hilda.

RAFE. Why not?

DAISY. Because she said something to me before tea which meant she would never do that.

RAFE. I see. (*To Wilfred*) Now, that just leaves you, then.

HAROLD. I don't think it was our Wilf.

RAFE (*moving up* c) How do you know?

HAROLD. Well, because . . .

WILFRED. Thanks, Harold. I was singing, Dad. You must have heard me. You all heard me singing, didn't you?

ARTHUR. Yes—I did, Wilf.

WILFRED. Thanks, Arthur.

HAROLD. So did I . . .

RAFE. Didn't I see you go into the kitchen?

WILFRED (*rising*) No, you didn't, I—oh, I'm sorry, I'm telling a lie. I did. Sorry, Dad. I went into the kitchen to get a drink of water —that was it. I remember now. (*He sits again*)

RAFE. You went to get a drink of water, just before your tea?

WILFRED. I always have a drink of water just before my tea, don't I, Mum? It gives me an appetite. You've seen me, haven't you, Harold?

HAROLD. Many a time. Come on, Mum, start pouring out the tea. We don't want an inquest on the herring.

RAFE (*to Harold*) It's an inquest on the truth. And don't you try to override me. (*To Wilfred*) Then you were the last in the kitchen?

WILFRED. I don't think so. 'Course I might have been. Was I, Mum?

DAISY. No, love, I think it was me.

WILFRED. There you are, Dad. I mean Mum wouldn't give the herring to the cat, and neither would I.

HILDA. I was last in the kitchen.

RAFE. You be quiet, please.

WILFRED (*rising*) I know that cat, Dad, it's a right thief. 'Course you can't blame 'em—it's in their nature. And they've got to follow their own natures.

Rafe (*moving down stage; to Wilfred*) Come here!

(Wilfred *rises and moves down* c. Daisy *touches his hand as he passes*)

I'm going to ask you a question. All I want to know is the truth, so be careful how you answer. Did you give that herring to the cat?
Wilfred. Me? Why should I? I didn't have to eat it, did I? Anyway, I like herrings. Don't I, Mum?
Daisy. 'Course you do, love.
Rafe. Answer me, did you give that herring to the cat?
Wilfred. I wouldn't do a thing like that, Dad. Would I, Mum? Knowing what store Dad had set on it.

(Arthur, *upset, is about to interfere, but* Florence *detains him.* Hilda *tries to persuade him with a look*)

Daisy. Of course you wouldn't love.
Rafe. Just hold your hands out, will you?
Wilfred. What—what for?
Rafe. Just put them out, please.

(*Only with difficulty can* Wilfred *get himself to hold out his hands.* Rafe *bends and sniffs at Wilfred's fingers.* Wilfred *looks very nervous.* Rafe *knows something, but keeps it to himself*)

Now, for the last time, answer me—did you give that herring to the cat?
Wilfred. Me? Certainly not! Positively not, as they say. I could swear to it—I could, honest . . .
Rafe. Oh—you could swear to it, could you? I see . . . (*He moves to the piano and picks up the Bible*)

(*Everyone watches Rafe with stunned amazement*)

Daisy. No—no—Dad—not the Bible—you can't make him . . .

(Rafe *waves Daisy and the others to silence.* Arthur *looks as though he might protest*)

Harold. This is not right, Mum.
Rafe. I'm going to get to the bottom of this. (*To Wilfred*) Take this holy book in your hand.
Wilfred (*aghast at the idea*) No, no, Dad, I couldn't. Don't ask me . . .
Harold. I think we've gone far enough.
Rafe. Take it when I tell you. Take it . . .
Wilfred. No—no, Dad . . .
Rafe. Take it! I never turn back once I start something. (*He thrusts the Bible on Wilfred*) Hold it up—up!

(Wilfred *looks to his mother*)

Wilfred. Mum—don't let him make me . . .

FLORENCE (*appealing*) Dad—you know you'll be sorry if you go too far.

RAFE. You can't go too far in finding the truth. (*Raising a hand for Daisy to be silent*) Now swear solemnly . . .

WILFRED. No! I can't.

ARTHUR. Don't press the lad any more, Mr Crompton.

(HILDA *watches Rafe with hatred.* RAFE *gives Arthur a look*)

RAFE. Be quiet, please.

FLORENCE. Wilf, love—say if you have . . .

RAFE. Now hold that book up—high—higher!

WILFRED. It would be wrong—swearing on God's Bible about a thing like that. Wouldn't it, Mum? Eh, Florence?

DAISY. Dad, don't force that good book on him. Let the lad tell you in his own way.

RAFE. He's told me in his way. I will not harbour a liar under my roof. (*Obsessively*) I must have the truth! It's the only way to live— by the truth.

DAISY. Don't press him too far, Dad—you know . . .

RAFE. I only want the truth. I'll not give way on that.

HILDA. Stop him, Mum—it's not right . . .

RAFE. Lift it up—up—higher. I'm determined to get the truth . . .

(WILFRED *holds the Bible up in trembling hands*)

Now say, I swear by Almighty God . . .

WILFRED. No! No! No, Dad . . .

HAROLD. You can't have a bloody inquisition over a herring.

RAFE. It's over nothing but the truth.

HAROLD. Then if you want to know the truth I'll tell you—I gave that herring to the cat.

WILFRED (*with a cry*) No! No, no, I must tell you—it were . . . (*He swoons*)

(*Everyone rises*)

HILDA (*with a scream*) Wilf! Mum, he's having one of his turns . . .

(RAFE *quickly catches Wilfred as he falls*)

DAISY. Don't let him fall . . .

RAFE. I've got him, Mother—now don't get excited. (*He slowly lets Wilfred down*) Open the window, somebody. Bring some cold water.

(ARTHUR *crosses* R *and opens the window.* HAROLD *exits to the kitchen for water*)

DAISY (*moving to* R *of Wilfred*) My little boy—he's all of a sweat. (*She kneels beside Wilfred. To Rafe*) You pressed him too far.

HILDA (*moving to above Wilfred*) Wilf, love—are you . . .

RAFE. He'll be all right—the water. (*He rises* L *of Wilfred*)

Daisy. I'll unfasten his collar . . .

Hilda (*to Rafe*) Oh, you—you—look what you've done to him—
(*picking up the Bible*)—you and your truth. I hate you—I could . . .
(*She raises the Bible to strike Rafe*)

(Florence *takes the Bible from Hilda and replaces it on the piano.*
Harold *enters with a glass of water*)

Oh, you brute—I'll not stay another minute under your roof. I'm
going, Mum. Take care of our Wilf. (*She kisses Daisy*) I'll never come
back to this rotten prison.

(Hilda *exits up* c, *slamming the door*)

Daisy. Hilda!

Harold (*handing Daisy the water*) Here y'are, Mum.

Daisy. He's coming round. Here, take this water, love.

(Rafe *comes back to himself after his shock*)

Rafe. Mind yourself, Mother—let me do it. You're spilling it.
(*He tends Wilfred, then hands the water to Harold*)

(Harold *exits to the kitchen with the water*)

Rafe. How do you feel, son?

Wilfred. Did I have one of my . . . ?

Daisy. Just a little one, love.

Wilfred. Let me get up. (*He rises*)

Rafe. Easy does it. Bide you there, where there's some air.

(Daisy *takes him to the sofa.* Rafe *moves the chairs in to make room*)

Wilfred. I thought I heard our Hilda shouting.

Rafe. Rest yourself, lad. Mother, shall we all get back to tea?

Daisy (*to Wilfred*) Will you be all right, love?

(Harold *enters from the kitchen*)

Wilfred. 'Course, I will Mum. It's a long time since I had one
of them. Carry on, everybody. Sorry about that herring, Dad. It was
me. I felt I couldn't bear to see it put in front of our Hilda again.

(*All except* Arthur *return to their places round the table*)

Rafe. It's all right—now you've told me. We'll not mention it
any more.

(Daisy *pours tea*)

Harold. Come on, Arthur, don't hang fire.

Arthur. Mother, don't pour any for me, please.

Daisy. Why not, love?

Rafe. Sit down, Arthur—and have your tea.

Arthur. No, thank you, Mr Crompton.

Harold. He'll have a cup of tea, Mum.

ARTHUR. No, I won't . . .

FLORENCE. Why—what's up, Arthur?

RAFE. I think he's got something on his mind.

ARTHUR. Yes, I have. What your Wilfred did—and your Hilda—they did out of love—love for one another—and they showed some spirit . . .

FLORENCE. Arthur!

ARTHUR. But you want to crush the spirit out of everybody who doesn't agree with you. You know what you are, Mr Crompton?

FLORENCE. Be quiet, Arthur.

ARTHUR. You're a bully.

RAFE. Oh . . . !

ARTHUR. Only a bully could have done what you've just done. (*To Daisy*) I'm sorry, Mother—I had to come out with it.

DAISY. All right, Arthur.

FLORENCE. I think you've said enough.

RAFE. Nay, don't stop him—I'm learning.

ARTHUR. You'll never learn—not so long as you ram your own way down everybody's throat. You make out you help 'em—but you only belittle 'em.

RAFE. Have you done?

ARTHUR. No. You used that Holy Bible for your own ends.

RAFE. I used it to find out the truth.

ARTHUR. The truth was staring you in the face—but you couldn't see it. You used it to satisfy your suspicious mind! My folk are nothing, but they would never even dare to do a thing like that. Yet you set yourself up as God-fearing! I used to respect you, but now I see you're nothing but a tyrant!

FLORENCE. Arthur!

ARTHUR. And another thing—you'd no right to let that little girl go off like that.

RAFE. Oh—why not?

ARTHUR. You wouldn't understand if I told you. (*To Daisy*) I'm right sorry, Mother. Good-bye, everybody. Florence, are you ready?

FLORENCE. Ready? What for?

ARTHUR. What do you think? To come with me.

FLORENCE. But I . . .

ARTHUR (*gently*) Now I'm afraid you'll have to make your mind up one way or the other. It's come to that.

(FLORENCE *looks at Rafe*)

RAFE. Aye, Florence, but you know what it'll mean if you go . . .

(FLORENCE *looks at Rafe, then at Arthur. She hesitates, then swiftly rises and picks up her jacket. She kisses Daisy and Wilfred, and puts her hand on Harold's shoulder*)

HAROLD. God bless, love.

FLORENCE *lets out an unexpected stifled sob and moves up* C. ARTHUR
takes her and exits with her up C, *as—*

the CURTAIN *falls*

SCENE 2

SCENE—*The same. Monday morning.*

*The downstage flap of the table has been lowered. The piano stool is
back in its usual place, the down* R *table chair below the sofa, and the down*
L *table chair* R *of the piano.*

When the CURTAIN *rises, the stage is empty. The radio is playing the final
tune of "Housewives' Choice". The front door is slightly ajar.* BETSY
JANE *is seen approaching it. She enters and calls.*

BETSY JANE (*off*) Daisy! Daisy! (*She appears in the doorway, calling
upstairs*) Daisy, are you there? (*She comes into the living-room*)

(DAISY *enters through the back door with her basket of washing and
dumps it on the washing-machine. "Housewives' Choice" finishes on the
radio. Sombre music is followed by a voice announcing, "It's five to ten".*
BETSY JANE *hurriedly switches it off.* DAISY *enters the living-room from
the kitchen*)

DAISY. Don't mind me. You're an early caller.

BETSY JANE. You left your front door open. Did you know?

DAISY. Yes, I'd a very special reason. Well, have you got my
five pounds?

BETSY JANE. You're not skint, are you?

DAISY. Yes, I am. (*She sits on the* R *arm of the* L *armchair*)

BETSY JANE (*coming down* C) Well, it's like this—Connie Clark's
mail order firm have let me down. I'd ordered a seven-day striking
clock with Westminster chimes from them, which should have
arrived this morning

DAISY. What's that got to do with my money?

BETSY JANE. I'd arranged to flog it to Mrs Clegg for five pounds
cash. It'll cost me seven pound ten, in instalments, of course, so it's
a bargain all round. But the damn thing hasn't arrived yet. It
might come by the afternoon post, and I swear on my dying . . .

DAISY. Don't swear! Just you bring it. I can't tell you the worry
it's caused me.

BETSY JANE. Leave it to me, Daisy, I'll not let you down. You
look tired.

DAISY. I didn't sleep all that well last night.

BETSY JANE. You're a clannish lot, you Cromptons!

DAISY. In what way?

BETSY JANE. You might have your troubles amongst yourselves, but you don't like it to go outside your four walls. You stick together as a family—I will say that for you.

DAISY. What are you getting at?

BETSY JANE. Your Hilda is just the same. She didn't want to say a word.

DAISY (*rising*) Is she all right? Have you seen her?

BETSY JANE. She's all right. Yon chap found her wandering about along the canal path. He brought her back and she spent the night with us. I got it out of her, though. Open confession is good for the soul. How you've been able to put up with that flaming husband of yours these past thirty years, I do not know! Mine's bad enough—but at least he's got the virtue of being stupid. I'll fetch her in. (*She moves to the front door and gives a whistling call off*) Come on, love, the coast is clear! (*She pokes her head into the room*) I'll leave you with her.

(BETSY JANE *exits and goes out through the front door.* DAISY *smoothes her face and hair to recover her motherly look.* HILDA *enters hesitantly, looks at Daisy, then runs into her arms, sobbing*)

DAISY (*hugging her*) There, there, there, are you all right, love? Ee, I'm right glad to see you.

(HILDA *breaks free and wipes her eyes*)

HILDA. I'm sorry, Mum, I am a softie.

DAISY. It'll do you good, love, a cry. Hold on a tick. Kettle's boiling.

(DAISY *goes to the kitchen.* HILDA *moves up to the door*)

(*From the kitchen*) So you didn't go to work today, love?

HILDA. No. Betsy Jane didn't wake me. I don't think I could have faced my mates at work if she had. I feel I can never face them again. You know, I used always be boasting about my dad.

(DAISY *enters with a small tray on which are two cups and a jar of instant coffee. She gives the tray to* HILDA)

DAISY. You'll get over it, love. How was it there at Betsy Jane's?

(DAISY *goes back into the kitchen.* HILDA *takes the tray to the pouffe down* L)

HILDA. They're a mucky lot, Mum. Good-hearted—ee, but I couldn't live there. She's got that enamel teapot on the hob beside the fire all the time. You can hear the tea sizzling and stewing inside. It would make you sick.

(DAISY *enters with a kettle of boiling water and a jug of milk*)

DAISY. Well, you get used to your own home. It's in the nature of things. (*She sits in Rafe's armchair*)

HILDA. In fact, I felt sick this morning before I even tasted it.

DAISY (*reacts*) Did you now!

HILDA. I hope my dad doesn't take that herring out on our Wilf.

DAISY (*making coffee*) You know your father never bears grudges —once he's rooted out things—except against himself. Our Florence went off with Arthur. I wish you'd seen that! It quite touched me. the courage he showed in standing up to your dad. I sometimes wish I'd shown a bit more. (*She holds out the kettle*)

HILDA (*placing the kettle in the fireplace and then sitting in the armchair* C) I don't know how you put up with him, Mum.

DAISY (*handing Hilda her cup*) You can always put up with somebody—so long as you know they're genuine.

HILDA. But look how he domineers you.

DAISY. Well, if he weren't doing that he'd be doing something else.

HILDA. And yet he used to be so understanding. I wonder what's made him change.

DAISY. Are you sure it's him that's changed, love?

(BETSY JANE *enters up* C)

BETSY JANE. It's only me. Oh, you've got the coffee on the go. (*She sniffs*) Doesn't it smell nice!

(DAISY *gives her a look then rises and goes to the kitchen*)

(*Moving* L *of Hilda*) Was she very upset?

HILDA. I haven't been able to tell her yet.

BETSY JANE. It'll give her a shock.

(DAISY *enters with a cup*)

DAISY. What's that?

BETSY JANE. Your Hilda has some news for you.

DAISY (*putting the cup on the tray and picking up the kettle*) Not bad, I hope? (*To Hilda*) What is it, love? (*She moves towards Hilda*)

HILDA (*rising and moving down* R) I'm getting out of it, Mum— I'm going away.

DAISY. Ee, for the moment I thought it was something worse.

HILDA. Worse? What?

DAISY. Nothing, love. Away? Where to?

BETSY JANE. She's going up to The Smoke—to London. (*She takes the kettle, fills her cup, and replaces the kettle*)

DAISY. Ee, you aren't, are you, love—going so far away?

HILDA. Yes, Mum, I'm going tonight.

BETSY JANE. Women bus conductors can earn fourteen pound a week.

DAISY. You don't want to go, do you, love, to London—a big strange city like that?

HILDA. I want to get away, Mum. I don't feel I can face folk here any more. I used to feel so proud of our home—but now . . .

BETSY JANE (*spooning coffee in her cup*) I've been telling her—she can't go to London without money in her pocket. (*She notices the sugar is absent, and fetches it from the kitchen*)

HILDA. Can you lend me some, Mum?

DAISY. Lend you—well, I'll have to scratch around a bit.

HILDA (*putting her cup on the table*) Don't worry, Mum, if you can't. I'll manage somehow. I've got my factory savings, but it takes a fortnight to get the money through. I'll go to Vy Hopkins—you know—who worked at our place. I can see you're worrying—now I'll manage one way or another. (*She takes two records from the rack down* R)

DAISY. Ee, love, I don't like the thought of it.

HILDA. I hate the idea—but I feel I must do it. Now I'll just go upstairs and collect a few bits of things.

DAISY. Aye, but leave some behind . . .

BETSY JANE. Just in case you change your mind.

HILDA. I'm not likely to do that.

DAISY. I shan't feel you're gone the same—if I see your things around.

HILDA. Don't worry about the money, Mum, if it's an awkward time.

(HILDA *exits up* c)

DAISY. Her father's favourite—and look what he's driven her to! (*Going to her handbag on the sideboard*) She can't go to London broke She must have something.

BETSY JANE (*putting her cup on the tray*) Aye, she'd be easy prey for all them pimps they've got down there—they're on the look-out for her sort.

DAISY. Do you think for certain you'll have that money for me today?

BETSY JANE. I hope so—but I couldn't say for certain. You know what the post is getting like these days.

DAISY. I've got to lay my hands on something for her. (*She moves to the desk and tries in vain to open it*)

BETSY JANE. Is there some money in there?

DAISY. Yes, quite a lot.

BETSY JANE. And you can't get at it? He's got the key, eh? (*She joins Daisy at the desk and tries to open it*) So near and yet so far.

DAISY (*moving* R) The girl's got to have some money. Do you know where I can borrow some?

BETSY JANE. Yes, but not without your husband's signature. They've got you every road. It's a man's world all right. (*Inspecting the lock*) Have you got a bit of wire? I might be able to pick this lock for you.

DAISY. What kind of wire?

BETSY JANE. Forget it—this hairpin will do. (*She begins to pick the lock*) I used to be quite good at it. My mother showed me how to do it. She used to say to carry out a wife's job you can't know too much.

DAISY. Is there anything I could pawn?

BETSY JANE. Would he miss the piano? (*She continues picking*)

DAISY. Here—what are you up to?

BETSY JANE. You're behind the times. There used to be fifty pawnbrokers in town, and now there's only two. They say there's more money about these days but it never comes my way. It's nothing when you have it, and all the world when you haven't.

DAISY. Here, be careful. Mind you don't scratch it.

BETSY JANE. I'd scratch him if I got half a chance. There is one pawnbroker I know—in fact I've my ring in hock there at present. I keep telling yon chap I've mislaid it. (*She chuckles*) Damn fools, men. You can tell 'em anything. I always feel it's a pity to tell 'em the truth. They don't believe you in any case.

DAISY. Leave it alone, please. I don't want you to tinker with it. Besides, you'll never open it.

(BETSY JANE *fiddles and tugs, and suddenly the lid springs open*)

BETSY JANE. You're too late! I bloody have. Practice makes perfect.

DAISY. Oh, my God!

BETSY JANE. All done by kindness, here's the lolly—(*She grabs the box, then picks it up with her apron*) Mustn't leave fingerprints.

DAISY. Put it back!

BETSY JANE (*crossing Daisy to the table*) Put it back!—are you mad? What about your Hilda? Besides, once I get my fingers on it I'll be able to pay you back the five quid I owe you. Now, where's the key for it?

DAISY (*searching in the desk*) The key! I forgot, he must have it with him.

BETSY JANE. Can you beat it! After all my trouble. It'll take two pounds of gelignite to bust this flamin' thing open.

DAISY (*turning with a paper-knife in her hand*) Can't you open it with a hairpin?

BETSY JANE. Hairpin? Who the hell do you think I am—Houdini? Give me that thing—it's got a sharp point.

DAISY (*giving Betsy Jane the paper-knife*) Go careful now.

BETSY JANE. What are you worried about—me or the bloody paper-knife?

DAISY. Don't ruin it.

BETSY JANE. If I had him here, I'd ruin him! (*She tries with the knife*) Dammit, it won't go in. (*She puts the knife down and raises the box above her head*) Stand back—I'll burst it open!

DAISY. No, no!

BETSY JANE. Don't get excited—I'm only coddin'.

DAISY. Quick, put it back, put it back!

BETSY JANE. What's up? What are you getting so nervous about? Anybody would think it was the holy of holies.

(DAISY *has a sudden realization of what she is doing, grabs the box and knife from Betsy Jane, puts them back in the desk and shuts the lid*)

DAISY. No! I can't bear the thought of what I'm up to.

BETSY JANE. It's what he's driven you to.

DAISY. Quick, lock it. He'd never forgive me.

BETSY JANE (*crossing to the desk*) Lock it? How can I? I've got no key.

DAISY. You opened it.

BETSY JANE. You can't lock 'em as easy. Now what are you going to do about your Hilda?

DAISY. There must be something I could give you to pawn as wouldn't be missed for a day or two—I could get round it somehow.

BETSY JANE. Well, it'll have to be summat special. Pawnbrokers are very choosey these days.

DAISY. Hold on a tick—I think I've got the very thing. Here, wait out the back for me—I don't want our Hilda to see.

(DAISY *exits up* C)

BETSY JANE. I wish I lived here. I'd have that box open if it were the last thing I did.

(BETSY JANE *exits to the kitchen, then enters the scullery and stands near the back door.* DAISY *hurries in carrying something on a coat-hanger which is covered with a white dust sheet.* BETSY JANE *waits near the back door as* DAISY *exits through the kitchen and into the scullery*)

Now what have you got there?

(DAISY *removes the dust sheet and holds up Rafe's new overcoat*)

Ee, that's a grand coat.

DAISY. How much do you think you could get me on it?

BETSY JANE. Whose is it?

DAISY. It's Rafe's. Never been worn. Only got it last Friday. Cost thirty-two guineas.

BETSY JANE. You're never going to pop it?

DAISY. Can you get me ten pounds on it?

BETSY JANE (*taking the coat*) Ee, it feels like velvet. He knows what's good—I'll say that for him.

DAISY. I durst not think of the shock he'd get if he knew I'd do a thing like this behind his back.

BETSY JANE (*rolling the coat up*) It might do him all the good in the world. It would let him see what scheming his wife has to do to get ten rotten quid for his daughter, and him having all that money locked away there under her nose. It's bloody men all over.

DAISY *pushes Betsy Jane out with the coat, as*—

the CURTAIN *falls*

Scene 3

Scene—*The same. Monday evening.*

When the Curtain *rises,* Wilfred *is seated at the piano playing a Chopin Nocturne.* Harold *is at the table* l, *very much aware of himself, brushing crumbs off the tablecloth into a crumb tray. There is a knock at the front door.*

Harold. Somebody at the door, Wilf.
Wilfred. Then why don't you go and answer it?
Harold. Me? I can't do two jobs at once. Besides, it might be our Hilda.

(Wilfred *stops playing and exits quickly up* c *to open the front door.* Harold *looks for somewhere to throw the crumbs, aims under the armchair* c, *then throws the tray in the sideboard drawer, folds the tablecloth carefully, concertinas it, and shoves it in the drawer.* Betsy Jane *enters up* c, *carrying a purse.* Wilfred *follows her)*

Betsy Jane. Is your mother in?

(Harold *places the runner and bowl of hyacinths on the table)*

Wilfred (*closing the door* c) She's washing up the tea things. Don't say you've brought that five quid back at last!
Betsy Jane. That's all been arranged between your mother and me.
Wilfred. Glad to hear it. I'll go and tell her you're here.

(Wilfred *exits to the kitchen)*

Betsy Jane (*sniffing*) There's a funny atmosphere in here.
Harold (*crossing down* l) Well, it was all right. (*He sits in the television chair* l *and picks up the evening paper)*
Betsy Jane. It feels like a morgue.
Harold. I wouldn't know. I've never been in one
Betsy Jane. Don't give up hope. (*She sits* l *of the table and looks round*) Where is he?
Harold. The old chap? He's upstairs. He's wandering about like a man lost.
Betsy Jane. That'll be a change.

(Wilfred *enters from the kitchen)*

Wilfred. She says you'd better go in to her.
Betsy Jane (*rising*) Right.

(Betsy Jane *exits to the kitchen)*

Harold. We could do with getting the old chap out of the way.

WILFRED (*moving* c) Aye, the girls'll be coming around. Can't you come up with something to get him out?

HAROLD. I'll try. You never think you'd miss 'em that much.

WILFRED. Aye, even our Florence! If it's only for her bossing.

HAROLD. Know what—I feel the time's getting ripe for us to move off with 'em—what do you say?

WILFRED. I'd say you were a bit too fond of Mum's cooking.

HAROLD. If I once set my mind on leaving, nothing will hold me. And it won't take much.

(WILFRED *sits at the piano and plays quietly.* HAROLD *goes back to his paper.* DAISY *enters the scullery with* BETSY JANE, *and they go to the back door.* DAISY *switches on the scullery light*)

BETSY JANE. I knew you'd be worrying.

DAISY. I'm glad you got the ten pounds for it.

BETSY JANE. Yes—but I only got nine pounds fourteen in cash. Know what they charge for a pawn-ticket on that amount? Five bob! Used to be tuppence.

DAISY. Thanks, Betsy Jane.

BETSY JANE. An' yon pawnbroker charges a shilling extra for putting the coat on a hanger—keeps the creases out, see. I thought he rated that. Count it to make sure it's right.

(RAFE *enters up* c, *wearing slippers and a cardigan. He sees Betsy Jane in the scullery, and sits in his armchair*)

DAISY. I trust you.

BETSY JANE. Thank you. Well, same as I say about the other, as soon as that Westminster chiming clock arrives I'll . . .

DAISY. Yes, I'd be very glad if you would.

BETSY JANE. Ee, Daisy, you look years older than when I came in last Friday tea-time.

DAISY. Yes—and I feel it.

BETSY JANE. Well, try not to worry. It'll not always be dark at seven. Has he tried his bureau yet?

DAISY. Don't remind me of it, I've enough on my mind.

BETSY JANE. Yon chap of mine isn't home from work yet. What pests men are! They're either missing from home or for ever under your feet!

(BETSY JANE *exits through the back door.* HAROLD *points at the paper.* WILFRED *turns his head and sees him*)

HAROLD (*reading the paper; excitedly*) Hi, Dad, you've missed something good tonight.

(DAISY *switches off the scullery light and goes into the kitchen.* WILFRED *stops playing and rises*)

RAFE. Have I now! What's that?

HAROLD The Messiah—at Manchester. Handel's Messiah.

Rafe. Nay, that's not tonight—that's Easter Monday.

Harold. Oh, no, Dad, it's tonight at seven-thirty—Huddersfield Choral Society. Look, there! What can't speak, can't lie (*He takes the paper to Rafe and points*)

Wilfred (*moving down to Harold*) By gum, you're right, Harold! Fancy that!

(*Daisy enters from the kitchen, switching off the light. She looks at the desk then crosses to the sideboard to put the money from Betsy Jane into her handbag*)

Rafe. I wish you'd told me earlier.

(*Wilfred moves up to the piano*)

Harold. You could still make it.

Daisy. You what?

Wilfred. The Messiah—at Manchester.

(*Daisy looks puzzled*)

Rafe (*rising and moving up c*) I thought it were next week, Mother. I don't know what's come over me lately. (*He hands the paper back to Harold*)

(*Harold sits again in the television chair l*)

I've got out suitcase down from the top of the wardrobe. When they come to collect their things you'll let me know, will you? I'd rather not be around.

Daisy. All right, Dad.

(*Rafe takes his bunch of keys from his pocket. Daisy watches apprehensively*)

Rafe. I expect you'll be needing some extra money now—with all this coming and going.

Daisy (*barring Rafe's way to the desk*) No, no, Dad—it's all right.

Rafe. Are you sure?

Daisy. Positive. I'll manage.

Wilfred. You could still get to Manchester in time, Dad.

Harold. Aye, Dad—there's a marvellous bus service. Better still, you could even catch a train . . .

Rafe (*moving to the fireplace*) I don't think I'll bother now.

Wilfred. You could be door to door in what—forty minutes.

Harold. Thirty-five with a bit of luck.

Rafe. You two seem to want to get me out of the way.

Harold. No, no. It's just that we know how you enjoy it.

Wilfred. It would take you out of yourself, Dad.

Rafe. What time did you say it starts?

Harold (*looking in the paper*) Seven-thirty. 'Course, they're always a bit late striking up.

Rafe. I think I will go after all. What d'you say, Mother? I'd like to get out.

DAISY. What's that, Dad?

RAFE   } *(together)* { The Messiah.
HAROLD }   { The Messiah—at Manchester.

DAISY (*moving down to* L *of Rafe*) Oh, I see. It might do you good, the change, Dad—but will you have time?

WILFRED (*cutting in*) 'Course he'll have time.

HAROLD. Sure he'll have time.

DAISY. Can I help you? You'll have to hurry.

RAFE. I'll just get the jacket to these trousers—and my black shoes.

WILFRED. I'll get your jacket, Dad.

(WILFRED *exits up* C)

HAROLD. Let me get your shoes, Dad.

(HAROLD *exits to the kitchen*)

DAISY. Is there anything you'd like me to say to them, Dad? When they come round? I mean—the girls.

RAFE. Aye, there's a lot, Mother—but I'm afraid nothing as would be of any use. Two good daughters—it takes you half a lifetime to bring 'em up—and you lose them in a couple of minutes. (*He goes quiet as the kitchen door opens*)

(HAROLD *enters with Rafe's shoes*)

HAROLD. It's better than seeing it on the telly, eh, Dad? (*He pulls Rafe's cardigan off and puts it on the chair down* R)

RAFE (*sitting on his chair to change his slippers*) Eh? Seeing it? Seeing's nothing—hearing's nothing. It's the participation. You've got to enter into the Messiah.

(WILFRED *enters up* C *with Rafe's jacket and puts it on the chair arm. Rafe puts on his slippers* L *of the chair.* DAISY *moves to the desk*)

HAROLD. Oh, I see what you mean, Dad.

(WILFRED *moves down* L)

RAFE. I don't think you do, lad. It's a going out of yourself and entering into a new world. I don't think you've tried it yet. (*He rises puts on his jacket and looks in the mirror* L)

DAISY. I'll get your coat, Dad.

(DAISY *exits up* C)

HAROLD (*looking out of the window* R) Aye, it'll be cold coming home.

WILFRED. Hy, Dad! A good idea—how about your new coat?

HAROLD. Good old Wilf! It'd be favourite tonight!

(DAISY *enters with Rafe's old coat, scarf and cap*)

What do you say, Mum?

DAISY. What's that?

WILFRED. My dad's new overcoat, don't you think he should wear it tonight?

RAFE. Stop fussing. I'll be all right as I am.

DAISY. Let your dad please himself.

WILFRED. I thought it'd be a good christening for it, Dad—the Messiah.

HAROLD (*moving up* C) Aye, a good idea, Wilf. I'll go and get it, eh, Dad? (*He opens the door wide*)

RAFE (*moving back to the fireplace*) Your mother's got me this one now. So shut up about the new overcoat.

HAROLD (*moving down stage*) Please yourself, Dad.

(DAISY *helps* RAFE *to put on his coat*)

RAFE (*adjusting the coat*) There's nowt wrong with this.

DAISY. P'raps you'll feel more at home in it. (*Moving up stage*) Now don't get yourself late.

WILFRED (*pointing*) Hy, Dad—you've got a button missing!

RAFE. Never! Where?

WILFRED. In the middle—look, right in the front.

RAFE. Bless my soul, so I have.

HAROLD. It's a sign, Dad. You should have put your new one on.

RAFE. Mother, what have you been up to?

DAISY (*moving down stage*) What? What do you mean?

RAFE. A button missing off my coat—that's not like you.

WILFRED. I'll run and fetch your new one, Dad.

RAFE. I'll be all right in this.

WILFRED. It'll not take me a tick, Dad.

RAFE. I tell you I'll be all right in this. Nobody's going to notice a button.

WILFRED. Sorry, Dad.

RAFE. You meant well, son. I'm sorry to bite your head off. Go on, off with you upstairs and fetch it.

WILFRED (*moving to* L *of Rafe's chair*) Right, Dad . . .

DAISY (*shouting*) No, no—don't go. It's no use.

(*They all go silent and look at her*)

HAROLD. What's no use?

RAFE (*taking off his coat*) What's up, Mother?

DAISY (*recovering*) It's no use him going—I'll go—I know where it is.

HAROLD. Let me go, Mum. Save yourself. (*He starts to move*)

DAISY. No! I tell you, no—why do you keep interfering?

(*They all go silent*)

RAFE. To save any bother, I'll go and get it myself. (*He gives his coat to Daisy, then turns*) Mother, you're not yourself this evening.

Keep calm—have faith. (*He gives her arm a comforting squeeze and moves slowly up* c)

(RAFE *exits up* c *to the stairs.* DAISY *watches after him.* WILFRED *and* HAROLD *look at her and then at each other*)

WILFRED. Mum, suppose I nip into Betsy Jane's and bring our Hilda back—soon as he goes?

(DAISY *does not appear to hear him*)

HAROLD. Aye, you do that Wilf.

WILFRED (*moving up* L) And you go down to Arthur's an' collect him an' our Florence. I'll get your jacket: (*He goes through to the scullery, collects his and Harold's jackets from the back door, and returns to the living-room*)

HAROLD. All right. (*He puts his arm around Daisy*) We'll go and see what's happening. We won't be long, Mum. I don't like to see you worried.

WILFRED. We'll nip back in the minute we see him go up the street.

RAFE (*off*) Where've you put it, Mother?

HAROLD. Now don't let yourself get upset, Mum.

WILFRED. It'll be all right.

RAFE (*off*) I can't see it.

DAISY. You go off now.

WILFRED. Not be long. God bless.

(WILFRED *and* HAROLD *put their jackets on, exchanging glances of concern*)

HAROLD. See you soon. It'll all come right.

(HAROLD *and* WILFRED *exit up* c *and through the front door*)

RAFE (*off*) Mother! Mother! Where have you put my new overcoat? It's not in the wardrobe. Can you come up and help me find it, love, or I'll be late.

(DAISY *moves about in desperation. She throws Rafe's clothes on the hallstand, grabs her handbag, throws it on the table, then crosses to the desk, flings the lid down, and covers her face*)

DAISY. I knew it! I knew I'd be found out! Oh, my God, what'll I do?

(RAFE *enters up* c, *carrying a dust cover and a hanger*)

RAFE. Mother, where's my new . . . (*He sees the desk open and places the cover and hanger on the chair up* c) What are you doing in my desk? Why is it open? What's been happening? And my coat missing? What's going on?

(DAISY *runs into Rafe's arms*)

Daisy. Oh, Rafe—hold me tight.

Rafe. I'll hold you, lass. There, there. Now, what's wrong? Tell me all about it.

Daisy. I can't. I can't bear to tell you.

Rafe. Surely you can tell me anything.?

Daisy. I needed some money.

Rafe. Go on.

Daisy. And I got Betsy Jane to break the lock open for me.

Rafe (*moving to the desk*) You needed money—then why didn't you come to me?

Daisy. It was for our Hilda—she's going to London tonight. But then your cash-box was locked and I didn't know what to do. I got desperate—so I pawned your overcoat instead. I had to get her some money. I'm so sorry!

Rafe. Why didn't you tell me?

Daisy. I couldn't. Then when you caught me at the desk I could see you looked so upset. Oh, Rafe . . .

Rafe. What happened to the housekeeping money?

Daisy (*sitting L of the table*) I wish I knew. Money has a funny way of slipping through my fingers.

Rafe. Money has a funny way of slipping through anybody's fingers—if they keep 'em open.

Daisy. I lent Betsy Jane five pound last Friday. They'd come to take her television away, and she didn't pay me back.

Rafe. So she opened my desk as a return favour. You still haven't told me why you didn't come to me for the money in the first place.

Daisy. Because I wanted you to go on thinking I was a good manager. I knew if I asked I'd have to explain a lot and all my faults would come out. I'm not what you think I am—I'm a very poor manager.

Rafe (*moving to L of Daisy*) Don't you realize that I love you for what you call your faults? I wouldn't want to change you for anything. As for your managing, I know more about that than you think. You wouldn't want two of my sort under one roof. I haven't made you go in fear of me, have I, lass?

Daisy. A bit. Your standards are too much for me. Over the week-end I got that I didn't know where to turn.

Rafe. It hurts me to hear you say that. It's the way my poor mother used to be and it's the one thing I was determined my wife would never be.

Daisy. Do try and forgive me, Dad.

Rafe (*kissing Daisy's forehead*) Nay, you must forgive me. I drove you to it. I try to do good by force, and force seems to blind a man. But the good you do, you do naturally, as though God were there with you.

Daisy. Don't say such things—you only upset me. Oh, but I'm so sorry about your lovely coat . . .

Rafe. I don't care a bloody damn about the coat—or the desk—

all I care about—all I've ever cared about—is you and our four children.

Daisy. I understand that.

Rafe. I know they don't thank me—but he'd be a poor father as went round looking for thanks from his children. A bit of love, happen, is as much as he can expect—if he's lucky. (*He takes his savings book and an envelope from the desk*) Our savings bank book, building society shares, ready cash for emergency. All this were here only for one purpose, so's we could pay our way in the world, and the family hold their heads up. Something I never knew in my childhood. Why, my poor mother hadn't a day's peace from bailiffs and tallymen. It was like a nightmare over the home. Every knock on our door was a threat. We daren't even answer it to a neighbour till we'd peeped through the curtains and made sure who it was.

Daisy. You never told me, Dad!

Rafe. It's not something a man wants to talk about. And I've never been one to seek pity. Going home from school I'd often spot a bailiff chap on the prowl. Then I'd have to sneak off and leave my mates and climb in over the backyard wall, making sure he wasn't following me. My mother would be waiting with a bundle of bedding to smuggle off to the pawnshop, or some scrap to take down to Aspinall's rag-and-bone yard. (*He sits in his chair*) I reckon that's why I went off at Arthur last Friday when he brought up old Aspinall— it must have all come back to me.

Daisy. Yes, I felt there was something.

Rafe. Worst of all, she used to try and keep all her debts hidden from my dad and she'd tell him one lie to cover up another, and then want me to bear her out. He never knew where he was. And in the end he could stand it no longer and he left us.

Daisy (*rising and moving to comfort Rafe*) Oh, Dad, I can't bear it.

Rafe. Now you know why I'm so obsessed about the truth. I know it's an obsession—but I just can't help it. I've never told you this before, but I came home from school one dinner-time and there were these two bailiff chaps sitting in our front room, playing cards, and when I went through into the back kitchen there was my mother—and she was trying to gas herself at the gas stove. That memory has never left my mind. I vowed that when I grew up I'd never owe a halfpenny. It might seem little enough to some folk to have paid their way, but I can't tell you the peace of mind it has given me. And whilst I might appear mindful of money, in my heart I despise it. No matter how much I may have to my name, the whole of it will never repay me one iota of all the misery I once suffered—aye, and those as were near me suffered—for the want of a few paltry shillings.

Daisy. If only the children knew—I'm sure they'd understand you better, Dad.

Rafe (*rising*) Oh, no—I'm not begging to be understood—not by my own flesh and blood. It'll come, in time, when they have families of their own to bring up. One night of tending a sick child will tell them more of what they have meant to me that any words of mine can. You have to go through your own lot before you can make sense of it all. We're none of us perfect, but we do our best. But I'll tell you this, Mother—(*he sits on the pouffe* L *and throws the savings book and envelope in the* L *firestool*) I'd sooner see this lot—savings, security and everything—flung behind the fire, rather than bring a moment's worry to you or drive any one of our children from their own home.

DAISY (*putting her arms round Rafe*) I know that, Dad, and I've always known it. But I'll tell you what I think—I think you might be happier from now on if you just took us as God made us. The more you love your children, the more you expect from them, and they can't always live up to it. Neither can I.

(RAFE *rises thoughtfully*)

RAFE. That reminds me, something's been troubling me all weekend. It's about our Hilda. (*He paces up and down* C)

(DAISY *watches him*)

DAISY. What about her?
RAFE. She always loved fried herrings.
DAISY. Yes, as much as I do.
RAFE. Now think back—wasn't there a certain time when you went off 'em?
DAISY. You don't mean . . .?
RAFE. I mean when you were pregnant.
DAISY. I could never face one then. But she can't be that way—not our Hilda! She's such an innocent.
RAFE. I know she is, bless her. And I keep saying it can't be that. But there's some change come over her. What do you know, Mother?
DAISY. I don't know anything. You can guess in these days. but I'll be honest—it has crossed my mind. But I've shut it out. Why, only this morning—but go on.
RAFE. What about this morning?
DAISY. Nothing.
RAFE. Well, if she is like that—I'll see to it the child is born under my roof and not on some dump in London. Let's say no more about it. I'm ashamed of myself now, for how I've been with her.
DAISY. In her heart she understands. But the trouble is, she's set on going to London tonight.
RAFE. I'll have to put a stop to that.
DAISY. But how?
RAFE. You leave it to me. There's more ways of killing a pig than cutting its throat. Besides, I've a suspicion that they might all join forces—I can smell rebellion in the air—but I'll think of some stroke. You've got to protect the young from themselves. (*He detaches two keys from his ring*) Here, you have these keys.

Daisy. I don't really need them now, Dad, I can always turn to you.

Rafe. I'd feel easier in my mind if you had them. I'd know for certain then you'd never be short.

Daisy (*taking the keys*) Thanks. And now I've something to live up to. Well, same as you say, let's not be too hasty about our Hilda. We don't know for sure.

Rafe. You know nothing for sure in this life. You can only grope your way along, holding on to your bit of faith and putting on the best front possible.

(WILFRED *and* HILDA *approach the front door, then hesitate and move away*)

Daisy. Well, you'd better put on a good one now, Dad, here they are.

Rafe (*moving up stage*) Right—I'll see you.

Daisy. Are you going upstairs?

Rafe. I don't think I could face them—not right now.

Daisy. You'll have to face them—sooner or later.

Rafe. Will I?

Daisy. Don't lose heart. And remember what you've always said —never humble yourself before your children, or it makes them start doubting.

Rafe (*picking up the dust cover and hanger*) I'll just go upstairs and rinse my face. And I'll remember that.

(RAFE *exits up* c. Daisy *looks after him, then hurriedly turns to collect the savings book and other things.* HAROLD *approaches the front door.* DAISY *goes to the desk, puts the things inside, and locks it.* HAROLD *enters as she does so*)

Harold. What are you doing in his desk, Mum?

Daisy. Minding my own business.

(WILFRED *enters up* c)

Wilfred. I've been watching for him—where is he?

Daisy. Your father? He's upstairs. Why?

Harold. How come he's not going out?

Wilfred. Has he had a change of mind?

Daisy. He's had more than that . . .

Wilfred. Is it safe fo 'em to come in?

Daisy. It's their home, isn't it? When hasn't it been safe?

(WILFRED *and* HAROLD *react and look at each other*)

Harold. Wilf, tell 'em to come in.

(WILFRED *exits up* c *to the front door*)

Are you sure you're all right, Mum?

Daisy. I think so. Why?

Harold. I don't know. I just wondered. You seem different. Oh, but wait till you hear our plans.

Daisy. What plans?

Harold (*moving up* c) All right. Come on in, then. (*He moves down* R)

(Florence, Hilda, Arthur *and* Wilfred *enter up* c. Daisy *hurries across to hug Hilda*)

Hilda. Oh, Mum, are you all right?

Daisy. Ee, love, I'm so glad to see you.

(Hilda *moves to the television chair and sits* L. Florence *kisses Daisy*)

Florence. Mother, we're bursting with news.

Arthur. Your Florence and I have decided to do it—at last.

(Wilfred *closes the door and moves to* L *of Harold*)

Wilfred. Do what?

Harold (*giving Wilfred a push*) Get married, you nit! What did you think!

Daisy. How nice!

Florence. Wednesday morning, Mum, by special licence.

(Arthur *gives Daisy a kiss on the cheek, and moves to the desk*)

Wilfred. D'you think it's worth it, Arthur?

Harold. Does he think what's worth it?

Wilfred. The extra expense of the licence.

Harold. He'll save that on the tax rebate.

Wilfred. I see—it might work out a bargain for him, together with the foreman's job. You certainly know your way about, Arthur.

Harold (*giving Wilfred a push*) Shut up, Wilfred. Know what—Mum—our Hilda's not going to London.

Hilda. No, but I'm not staying at home. I've arranged to go and stay with Betty Partington until I get things sorted out.

Wilfred. Well, keep your suitcase locked in that household.

Harold. Wilf, stop butting in! And break our news to Mum.

Wilfred. What news? Oh, yes—we've all planned to leave home.

Harold. Aye, we're getting out at last, Mum.

Daisy (*sitting in Rafe's chair*) Why not? Home's the place you can always come back to when nobody else wants you.

Florence (*moving* R *of Daisy*) And we're all set for you to come and live with Arthur and me—after what happened yesterday.

Daisy. I've stood thirty years of yesterdays, love—one sort or another. Now what about your dad? What's been arranged for him?

Wilfred. We never gave him a thought.

Daisy. Never gave your dad a thought . . . ?

HAROLD. Let him have the blooming house to himself—see how he gets on then.

HILDA. Don't talk like that about leaving Dad alone—in spite of what he drove you to, Mum.

DAISY. What do you mean—drove me to?

HILDA. Betsy Jane told me on the quiet—how you had to pawn his new overcoat.

DAISY. Sssh—sssh!

HAROLD. His thirty-two guinea overcoat in pop! I don't believe it!

WILFRED. You haven't really put it in uncle's!

DAISY. Yes, I had to. I needed the money for our Hilda, and I'd nowhere to turn.

WILFRED. Just fancy, and we were yapping away for him to put it on.

HAROLD. *You* were!

FLORENCE. Does he know?

DAISY. Yes, I told him everything.

(*They look at one another in wonder*)

HAROLD. He'll never come down them stairs alive.

HILDA. What did he say, Mum?

FLORENCE. What did he say!

DAISY. I'll tell you what he said. He said he was sorry and asked me to forgive him.

HAROLD. By heck, he must have changed a hell of a lot in the last five minutes—if he said forgive me!

(*There is a knock at the front door*)

WILFRED. Somebody at the door, Harold.

(HAROLD *starts to move up to open the door, caught unaware in the moment of confusion. Then he raises his fist at Wilfred for having caught him, and continues his move to exit up* C)

DAISY. And what's more, he gave me these. (*She holds up the keys*)

WILFRED. The keys to his desk?

FLORENCE. He didn't, did he? (*She sits on the arm of the armchair* C)

HILDA. I don't believe it.

(HAROLD *enters up* C *with* BETSY JANE. HAROLD *moves down* R, L *of Wilfred.* BETSY JANE *moves down* C)

BETSY JANE. It's only me.

DAISY. What is it, Betsy Jane?

BETSY JANE (*dipping into her bag*) Yon fellow had a big win on the horses—he's just come home drunk, and I've been through his pockets already. So here's two pounds off what I owe you. Pay your debts and you can come again.

HAROLD. You haven't paid 'em yet.

WILFRED. Don't forget there's another three quid.
BETSY JANE. You shut up, Here you are, Daisy.
DAISY. No thanks.
BETSY JANE. What's up?
HAROLD. She wants all or nothing.
DAISY. I don't want to touch the money.
HAROLD. Have you gone out of your mind, Mum?

(*The others murmur in surprise*)

DAISY. No! But on one condition—that you never come to me to
borrow another ha'penny.
HAROLD. But five pounds, Mum!
WILFRED. She might never see the other three.
FLORENCE. It's a lot of money just the same.
DAISY. It'll have been worth it for the change it's brought my
life.
FLORENCE (*rising*) But, Mother . . .
ARTHUR (*cutting in*) I see your mother's point. She wants her
peace of mind. So let her have it.

(FLORENCE *moves above Daisy to* R *of Arthur*)

DAISY. That's it, Arthur.
BETSY JANE. Of course, if you'd rather not take it, I understand.
(*Quickly returning the money to her bag*) It'll mean I'll have to find an-
other neighbour to tap—because I'll never have the nerve to come to
you again.
WILFRED. You'll get the dirty kick-out if you do.
HILDA. You keep out of it—you won't be here.
WILFRED. How do you mean—I won't be here?
HAROLD. You're leaving home, didn't you know?
WILFRED. Oh, I'd forgot!
BETSY JANE. Ee, Florence, I think it's a crying shame things
should have come to this pass for your poor mother—the entire
family going at one swoop. Still, I'd love to see your father's face
when he gets home from his Hallelujah Chorus.
HAROLD. He's not gone.
BETSY JANE. Then where the hell is he—out on the booze?
ARTHUR. Mr Crompton's upstairs.
BETSY JANE. Upstairs! Sufferin' Alice! Why didn't somebody
warn me? I'm off! Excuse me, everybody, but I don't want to meet
him. I might tell him a few home truths. (*She hurries to the door up* C)

(RAFE *enters up* C *as* BETSY JANE *reaches it.* BETSY JANE, *waving
behind her, does not see him, until she turns and collides with him*)

Oh—Mr Crompton—I do beg your pardon—I—I'm just off . . .

(RAFE *looks at her keenly, then stoops to pick up a hairpin*)

RAFE. Hy, just a tick, missis—you've dropped something.

BETSY JANE. It's only a hairpin.

RAFE. Aye, but you never know when you might need it. Here y'are. Good night—and go careful now.

(BETSY JANE *takes the hairpin and stares, fascinated, at Rafe as she exits speechlessly.* RAFE *comes down* C, *approaching the silent group.* ARTHUR *looks to the others for someone to speak*)

ARTHUR (*getting no help*) She's a rum 'un.

RAFE. Aren't we all—in our different ways. Arthur, I've been thinking over some of those things you said to me yesterday tea-time.

ARTHUR (*moving above Daisy's chair to* L *of Rafe*) So have I. Did I overstep the mark?

RAFE. Nay, never regret having spoken your mind. I only wish I'd done it more often.

(HAROLD *and* WILFRED *react*)

ARTHUR. Oh! Me an' your . . . your Florence and I thought of getting married.

FLORENCE (*putting her arm through Arthur's*) Thought! We are!

ARTHUR. Oh, aye—sorry, Flo—Wednesday morning—by special licence.

RAFE. It shouldn't be a rush job, but as St Paul says, it's better to marry than burn. Mother, find out the number of guests and go down to the Co-op restaurant first thing in the morning. Order the best breakfast they do. Don't mind the cost, Arthur. I can pay for it.

ARTHUR. No, I'm sorry—you can't—I mean we aren't—Florence . . . !

FLORENCE. We aren't thinking of getting married from here, Dad.

RAFE. Why—where else would you get married from, lass—but your own home?

DAISY. She thought of getting married from Arthur's mother's.

RAFE. Did she? Well, she can't.

ARTHUR. What do you mean, Mr Crompton—"she can't"?

RAFE (*patting Arthur on the shoulder*) Listen, Arthur, you've won one round—don't let it go to your head. You don't have a bride and groom going out of the same front door, and travelling in the same cab to their wedding, do you?

ARTHUR. I hadn't thought of that.

RAFE (*to Florence*) And do you realize the years your mother must have looked forward to this occasion—to the day she'd see her eldest daughter go out that door a bride?

DAISY. Our Florence had planned to stay these next nights at Arthur's.

RAFE. Our Florence can't stay these next nights at Arthur's. One night away from home is quite enough before marriage. You don't want to go making a habit of it.

FLORENCE (*moving to Daisy and taking her hand*) Of course, Arthur, if Dad thinks it's the proper thing to do—to marry from here . . .

ARTHUR. Aye, well yes, it will save us moving your bags . . .

(FLORENCE and ARTHUR *move up* LC)

RAFE. Is there anything else, Mother, while we're about it? (*He nods to Daisy, indicating Hilda*)

DAISY (*rising*) Our Hilda——

(HILDA *rises*)

—I think we must tell your dad now—(*moving towards Hilda*) she's set on leaving home.

RAFE. Leave home, eh? What a wonderful thought! I envy you.

HAROLD. She's not the only one that's going.

(RAFE *turns slowly*)

I'm going an' all. (*Nudging Wilfred*) And him.

WILFRED. Oh? What? Yes!

HAROLD. And we're going tonight.

RAFE. You know something—you should have done it years ago. Think of the freedom! How I envy you all! I only wish I could leave home—just like that. What do you say, Mother?

DAISY. It must be nice—having the choice.

HILDA (*crossing below Daisy*) I'll just go upstairs and collect the rest of my things (*She moves towards the door up* C)

RAFE (*stopping her*) I'll miss you, love—I'll miss all of you—but I don't blame you. The times I've reached that top corner on my way home from work and have thought to myself, if only I had the guts to turn the other way—to get away from it all, start life afresh somewhere. But I've always lacked the courage.

WILFRED (*accusingly*) You never wanted to leave us, did you, Dad?

(*The others stiffen.* HILDA *moves back below Daisy to* L)

RAFE. I'm only human—I wasn't born married. Why, I was only thinking last Friday teatime as I came through that door—there'll be our Harold taking the mickey, our Hilda in one of her moods, and there'll be Mother, bless her, with that frozen look of honesty she puts on her face after the last-minute fiddling of the housekeeping accounts. Florence, I don't know what it'll be like now that you're going.

DAISY. Oh, Dad, don't say you knew all the time!

RAFE. Over the years I've hardly been able to keep a straight face going through your figures. Know what the window-cleaning has cost this past month? Two pounds fourteen and ninepence! It's a wonder there's any glass left!

DAISY. It's a pity after keeping quiet all this time you had to come out with it just now.

RAFE. Well, we were all putting a front on, weren't we? But now we've got to put our house in order, so in the future let's have no more secrets from one another. Out with everything.

HAROLD. O.K., I'll make a start now. (*He deliberately lights a cigarette*)

DAISY. Dad, I think you'd better take your keys back.

RAFE. Why? What for?

DAISY. I feel I'm not cut out for cashier. I'm a rotten reckoner.

RAFE. But you're in sole charge now. You won't have to reckon —you'll just have to spend. You've nobody to answer to but yourself.

DAISY. Oh, yes, I'd forgot—and there'll only be the one pay packet every Friday. It'll be easy. (*She smiles round at the doleful faces*) No borrowing, no lending—with just the two mouths to feed.

WILFRED. And the cat! Don't forget him.

RAFE. He'll not go hungry.

DAISY (*dangling the keys*) Well, if you change your mind . . .

RAFE. Nay, I'm not likely to—I've come to realize that anything you have to lock away with a key just isn't worth the worry. And, same as they say, the home will be here when we're gone. I'll go and get my coat.

DAISY. Why—you're not going out, are you?

RAFE. I thought you might like to say good-bye to one another in peace.

WILFRED. You're not in our way, Dad. Is he?

ARTHUR. No—not at all.

RAFE (*moving towards Wilfred*) Thanks, lad, very good of you, I'm sure. But I need some fresh air. And I dare say you've a lot to talk over. (*He stops in front of Harold and looks at the cigarette*)

(HAROLD *reacts with nervous bravado.* RAFE *is unexpectedly gentle*)

Forgetting your manners, son? Pass them round, can't you?

(RAFE *exits up* C *for his coat.* DAISY *moves up* C)

WILFRED. You heard what he said!

(WILFRED *and* ARTHUR *go to get their cigarettes from Harold.* HAROLD *stubs his cigarette out*)

WILFRED. What's up?

HAROLD. I didn't like the way he said it. What's come over him, Mum?

ARTHUR (*rejoining Florence*) He seems quite different.

WILFRED. Aye, he's not like his normal self.

HAROLD. I never knew he had one.

WILFRED. I've a feeling he's up to something.

HILDA. I think it's very irresponsible of him to pick a time like this to go out—with so much to be settled.

FLORENCE (*moving to* R *of Hilda*) Oh, you shut up—you caused it all.

HILDA. Me!

FLORENCE. Why didn't you eat that bloody herring!

(*They all look at Florence in astonishment.* HILDA *sits in the television chair* L. RAFE *enters up* C *with his coat and cap*)

RAFE. Mother, do you remember the morning we got married?

DAISY. Yes, I'll never forget it. I can see you this minute, standing there at the altar at St Philip's Church, and the organ playing. Why?

RAFE. You'd never have imagined then, with all the years ahead, and being blessed by a family, that the time would come when they all suddenly clear off and leave you over a single week-end. And that we'd end up all on our own, more or less the same as we started.

DAISY. Aye, except a flamin' sight older, uglier—and wiser!

RAFE. I only hope it never happens to any of you. It can be a nasty wrench.

(*The others appear affected by this.* RAFE *moves to Arthur and shakes his hand, then goes to kiss Florence and wish her luck. Meanwhile,* DAISY *moves to between Wilfred and Harold*)

DAISY. Somebody's got to stop him going out.

HAROLD. Why?

DAISY. Your father's not himself. Anything could happen.

WILFRED. Aye, he might never come back. He could go from one extreme to another. They do, y'know—his sort. And you heard what he said about wanting to leave us all in the lurch.

HAROLD (*moving up stage*) You leave it to me, Mum. I'll put the block on him.

RAFE (*beckoning to Daisy as he is about to go*) Mother, I'm off . . .

(HAROLD *blocks Rafe's way at the door*)

HAROLD (*standing up* R *of Rafe at the door*) Just a moment, Father.

RAFE. What is it?

HAROLD. I'd like a word with you.

RAFE. What about?

HAROLD. About this upheaval.

WILFRED. Which upheaval?

HAROLD. Blimey, have you forgot again? You're leaving home!

WILFRED. Sorry—it had slipped my mind.

HAROLD. How many more times do I have to tell you?

ARTHUR. Don't forget you'll both have to find lodgings for the night.

WILFRED. So we shall.

HAROLD. Lodgings! That side of it never struck me!

WILFRED. Why, did you think we could walk the streets all night?

RAFE (*to Harold*) You were saying?

HAROLD. One moment, Father . . .

WILFRED (*to Harold*) Do you know anybody who'll take us in?

HAROLD. How should I know? I've never been a vagrant. Do you know anybody, Mum?

DAISY. No, love, I don't. Ask your dad.

HAROLD (*beckoning*) Wilf . . .

WILFRED (*moving to R of Harold*) Dad, you don't know anybody who'd take me and our Harold in, do you?

RAFE. No, not just like that. They nearly all want references these days. 'Course your mother would give you one. What were you after—full board, bed and breakfast, or just your kip for the night?

(WILFRED *and* HAROLD *look at each other bewildered*)

WILFRED. I never knew it was such a business.

DAISY. I suppose at a pinch they could get in at the Salvation Army hostel.

RAFE. Aye, they're not too particular.

ARTHUR. Ee, I don't think they'd like it there.

RAFE. Not to worry—they'll find something.

FLORENCE. I just can't imagine the home without our Wilf and Harold.

(WILFRED *looks sad*)

ARTHUR. Aye, they were like fixtures, so the place is bound to seem empty.

WILFRED (*to Harold*) Well, come on, it's getting late. And we've nothing packed yet.

HAROLD. Now you don't want to be too rash, Wilfred . . .

WILFRED. Me—rash! How do you mean?

HAROLD. It's all right making your bid for freedom—but you've got to think of Mother and the home. You were born in this house. Remember.

WILFRED. No, I don't!

RAFE (*to Harold*) You were saying?

HAROLD. Yes, Father, I've been thinking things over. What say we all hung on and gave it another go—pull together, like?

ARTHUR. Good idea—bury the hatchet!

WILFRED. I'm willing—if everybody else is.

(WILFRED *and* HAROLD *brighten up*)

FLORENCE. Yes, it seems such a pity to split up.

WILFRED. Aye, especially at a time like this—just when we're getting to know each other.

HAROLD. What do you say, Mum?

DAISY. Your dad and I have no choice. It's all been the one go for us ever since our family came along. Eh, Dad?

RAFE. Aye, you're tied to your children—even if they're not to you. But now I feel it's all come to an end.

(*The others murmur in surprise*)

HAROLD. How do you mean?

FLORENCE. In what way?

RAFE. It wouldn't work any more. I've come to see our Hilda was right.

WILFRED. How?

RAFE. A home can be a prison where there isn't love.

HILDA (*rising*) I never meant it like that.

DAISY. Of course she didn't.

RAFE. No matter how well it's run.

FLORENCE. You've got it wrong, Dad.

RAFE. Nay, I must have failed you. Sorry. God bless, everybody. (*He turns to the door*) I'm off.

HILDA. I tell you I didn't mean it that way!

HAROLD. Now steady up, Dad. (*He detains Rafe*) Don't be too hasty.

ARTHUR. Love, Mr Crompton—why, there's any God's amount of love in this house! Even I can see that.

WILFRED. 'Course there is.

FLORENCE (*putting her arm through Arthur's*) Always has been.

DAISY. Surely you knew that, Dad?

RAFE. Well, I've had my doubts of late.

WILFRED. I'm not surprised.

(HAROLD *digs Wilfred to shut up*)

HAROLD. It's just that we've a funny way of showing it.

WILFRED. Aye, that's it.

DAISY. Happen we're a funny lot.

(RAFE *surveys them*)

RAFE. Yes, I see what you mean.

DAISY. But when you get down to it, what family isn't?

WILFRED. And it's a poor home that won't stand the odd row.

HAROLD. Shut up! (*He takes Rafe's cap and coat*)

(FLORENCE *and* ARTHUR *move to the desk*)

Well, now the air's been cleared, what say we stick around and have another bash—eh, Wilf?

WILFRED (*crossing R below Daisy*) I suppose we could go farther and fare worse.

DAISY. You could, for sure. (*Crossing below Harold to Rafe*) But what about you, Dad?

RAFE. You know me, I'm easy. Will somebody put the kettle on?

(RAFE *and* DAISY *go to each other*)

WILFRED. Harold, the kettle!

(HAROLD *turns towards the kitchen, then catches on and raises his fist at Wilfred*)

HILDA. Dad . . . !

HILDA *walks below Florence and Arthur towards Rafe, as—*

the CURTAIN *falls*

FURNITURE AND PROPERTY LIST

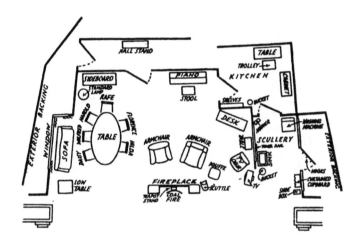

ACT I

On stage: LIVING-ROOM

Sofa (R) *On it:* cushions

6 dining chairs, one with arms (round table RC)

Armchair with chintz covering (C)

Armchair, leather (LC) *On it:* newspaper

Television chair (L)

Pouffe (L)

Oval table with flaps (RC) *On it:* tablecloth

Occasional table (down R) *On it:* gramophone

Record rack (L of gramophone table) *In it:* 12 record covers

Occasional table (L) *On it:* workbasket with scissors, sock, needle, darning wool; vase of daffodils; paperback book

Desk (up L) *On top:* table lamp, clock, family photograph, 2 letters. *Inside, on flat surface:* cash-box and coins in tray, paper-knife. *In drawer:* union rule book. *In compartments:* shares, envelopes, savings book

Sideboard (up R) *On it:* radio, bowl of hyacinths, table runner (folded), crumb tray and brush, Daisy's handbag (with notes, loose pennies, purse and coins, cash-book with pencil attached). *In drawers:* 6 fish knives and forks, 6 teaspoons, 6 napkins in rings, 1 folded napkin. *In cupboards:* salt, pepper, sugar, jampot and spoon, chutney

Piano (up RC) *On top:* 12 books between book-ends, including bound poetry volumes, family Bible, bust of Handel

Piano stool. *In seat:* large music book

Television set (down L) *On it: Bolton Evening News, TV Times, Radio Times*

In fireplace: firestools, fire-irons, teapot stand, coal glove, scuttle

On wall above desk: mirror

Carpet

Hearth-rug

KITCHEN

Table (up C) *On it:* tray with biscuit tin, coffee jar, 2 cups and saucers, 1 spoon, plate and piece of cake, cup of tea, sandwiches on plate in napkin, teapot and fresh tea

Trolley (below table) *On it:* 6 cups and saucers, jug of milk, 6 plates of herring with mashed potato and tomato

Cabinet (L) *In it:* 6 side plates, butter dish, tartare sauce, saucer, 2 plates of bread-and-butter, apple pie, chocolate cake, Sunday teapot

Shelves (down L below door) *On them:* glass of water, plate and prop herring, ashtray, Rafe's slippers, dummy cat (if used)

SCULLERY

Hoover cleaner (up R)

Washing machine (up L)

Sink (down R) *In it:* soap in dish. *Over it:* small mirror

Plastic bucket (below sink)

Towel rail (above sink) *On it:* towel

Curtained cupboard (down L below back door)

On floor down L: shoe-box and duster

CORRIDOR

Hall-stand. *On it:* Rafe's old coat and scarf

Off stage: Briefcase. *In it:* exercise books, clutch bag containing spectacles, note, wage packet (£8), pencil (FLORENCE)

Cat (WILFRED)

Shoulder-bag. *In it:* wage packet with £5 note, handkerchief (HILDA)

Weekend magazine (HILDA)

Thermos and lunch-box (RAFE)

Bolton Evening News (RAFE)

Large box, tied with string, containing overcoat wrapped in tissue paper, and bill in envelope (FLORENCE)

Personal: WILFRED: wage packet (£7 10s.), comb
           HAROLD: bicycle clips, cigarettes and lighter, wage packet (£6),
              £1 note in back trousers pocket
           RAFE: keys on chain, wage packet (3 £5 notes, 5 £1 notes, coins),
              pen
           ARTHUR: cigarettes

ACT II

SCENE 1

Strike: *Weekend* magazine
         Hilda's handkerchief
         Florence's briefcase and contents
         Bolton Evening News
         Letter from desk
         Wilfred's boiler suit
         Dishes, etc., from trolley
         Arthur's teacup and plate
         Arthur's cap

Set: Curtains open
        News of the World on TV chair
        Table chairs around table
        Piano stool down L of table
        Bowl of flowers and runner on sideboard
        Workbasket on small table L
        Poetry book on Rafe's armchair
        £5 note and 5 £1 notes on top in cashbox
        3 £1 notes in Daisy's bag
        Hilda's mac on hall-stand
        Dummy cat (if used) in basket with lid, above TV chair
        On table RC (false top): 6 large knives and forks, 1 fish knife and fork,
           7 butter knives, 5 side plates (no side plates on the two upstage
           places), 7 napkins, salt, pepper, sugar bowl, tartare sauce, chutney,
           plate of bread and butter

    KITCHEN

    On table: Act I sugar bowl, cup, saucer and spoon
    On trolley: (Sunday china), 7 cups and saucers, milk jug, 3 plates of
       apple pie, 6 plates of salad, 1 empty plate
    In cabinet: chocolate cake, sandwiches in napkin, teapot

Off stage: Sprig of white heather (RAFE)
            Herring bone (RAFE)

Scene 2

Strike: False table top with tea things
      Trolley, to kitchen

Set: Downstage flap of table lowered
      Piano stool to piano
      Downstage L dining chair to R of piano
      Downstage R dining chair to below sofa
      Window closed

      KITCHEN
      Kettle to boil
      Jug of milk

Off stage: Basket of washing (DAISY)
      Rafe's new overcoat covered with dust sheet, on hanger (DAISY)

Personal: BETSY JANE: hairpins

Scene 3

Strike: Coffee things
      Washing basket

Set: *Bolton Evening News* on TV chair
      Harold's and Wilfred's jackets on scullery door hooks
      Rafe's old coat (with button missing), scarf and cap on hall-stand
      Rafe's shoes in kitchen
      Cloth on table
      Crumb tray and brush on table, for Harold
      Hairpin on floor up C

Off stage: Dust cover and hanger (RAFE)

Personal: BETSY JANE: purse with £5 note, 2 £1 notes, coins

LIGHTING PLOT

Property fittings required: LIVING-ROOM: pendant, standard lamp (up R), desk lamp

KITCHEN: pendant

SCULLERY: hanging light

Interior. Composite set, living-room, kitchen, scullery. The same scene throughout

THE APPARENT SOURCES OF LIGHT are, by day, a window R; by night, pendants and lamps

THE MAIN ACTING AREAS are RC, C, down C, LC, down L

ACT II Early evening

To open: Effect of fading evening light

Cue 1	BETSY JANE enters	(Page 2)
	Start Slow fade to dusk	
Cue 2	WILFRED switches on scullery light	(Page 6)
	Snap on scullery lighting	
Cue 3	FLORENCE switches on living-room lights	(Page 7)
	Snap on pendant and desk lamp	
Cue 4	HILDA switches on standard lamp	(Page 10)
	Snap on standard lamp	
Cue 5	DAISY: "that'll kill it."	(Page 10)
	TV light flickers on	
Cue 6	DAISY switches on kitchen light	(Page 10)
	Snap on kitchen lighting	
Cue 7	RAFE turns TV off	(Page 11)
	TV flicker fades to off	
Cue 8	FLORENCE switches off kitchen light	(Page 14)
	Snap out kitchen lighting	
Cue 9	DAISY switches on kitchen light	(Page 23)
	Snap on kitchen lighting	
Cue 10	DAISY switches off kitchen light	(Page 24)
	Snap out kitchen lighting	

ACT II, SCENE 1. Afternoon

To open: Effect of late afternoon light

Cue 11	DAISY: "Peace in the home at last."	(Page 37)
	Start slow fade to dusk	
Cue 12	FLORENCE switches on living-room lights	(Page 40)
	Snap on pendant and desk lamp	

Cue 13   HILDA switches on standard lamp   (Page 41)
         Snap on standard lamp

ACT II, SCENE 2. Morning
To open: Effect of morning light
No cues

ACT II, SCENE 3. Evening
To open: All living-room and kitchen lighting on. Scullery off
Cue 14   DAISY switches on scullery light   (Page 56)
         Snap on scullery lighting
Cue 15   DAISY snaps off scullery light   (Page 56)
         Snap out scullery lighting
Cue 16   DAISY switches off kitchen light   (Page 57)
         Snap out kitchen lighting

EFFECTS PLOT

ACT I

ACT II

SCENE 1

SCENE 2